"Through the prism of working-class self-organization, Mariarosa Dalla Costa traces the historical development of the welfare state in the United States. She details the ways in which the family was instituted as the basic unit of social organization and the role bestowed upon women in the reproduction of labor power. Widening the lens, Dalla Costa maps the broader configurations of gender, race, and class that the welfare state was built upon to reveal its systematic exclusions. *Family, Welfare, and the State* is an important book for a time when we confront the fallout of neoliberal restructuring. Against nostalgia, the current challenge is not to return to the past, but to struggle for a better future." —**Emma Dowling**, author of *The Care Crisis: What Caused It and How Can We End It?*

"Mariarosa Dalla Costa's landmark study of working-class struggles and the US state in the early decades of the twentieth century vividly illustrates how capitalist development passes through both family and home. The Great Depression, Dalla Costa argues, involved a massive crisis in the social reproduction of labor-power. She shows how militant movements by unemployed and employed workers prompted the New Deal state to intervene directly in the domestic sphere, inventing new norms for "women's work" along the way. This prehistory of the welfare rights and wages for housework movements will remain essential reading for activists and scholars in the twenty-first century and beyond." —**Andrew Anastasi**, editor and translator of *The Weapon of Organization: Mario Tronti's Political Revolution in Marxism*

"Dalla Costa's analysis of the New Deal is essential reading for contemporary theorists of racial patriarchal capitalism. Centered on the nexus of the state, the family, social reproduction, and popular struggles in a period of dramatic change, *Family, Welfare, and the State*'s historically situated argument feels prescient. Dalla Costa's feminist analysis of the Keynesian *prequel* to neoliberalism, which attends to the crisis of waged work and social reproduction in the 1930s, is critically important to our present imagination of—and struggle against —neoliberalism's sequel." —**Kathi Weeks**, author of *The Problem with Work: Feminism, Marxism, Antiwork Politics, and Postwork Imaginaries*

FAMILY, WELFARE, AND THE STATE

Originally published in Italy as *Famiglia, welfare e stato tra Progressismo e New Deal* in 1997 by FrancoAngeli, Rome.

Translated from Italian by Rafaella Capanna

"On Welfare (1977–1978)" was originally published in *Primo Maggio: saggi e documenti per una storia di classe* 9–10 (1977–1978): 76–80. It appears here in translation by Richard Braude and in Mariarosa Dalla Costa's *Women and the Subversion of the Community* (PM Press, 2019). Reprinted with permission from PM Press.

ISBN: 978-1-94217-353-3 | EBook ISBN: 978-1-94217-359-5
Library of Congress Control Number: 2021942966

Common Notions   Common Notions
314 7th Street   210 South 45th Street
Brooklyn, NY 11215   Philadelphia, PA 19104

www.commonnotions.org
info@commonnotions.org

Cover design by Josh MacPhee/Antumbra Design
Layout design and typesetting by Morgan Buck/Antumbra Design
www.antumbradesign.org

Special thanks to Bryan Welton for editorial assistance.

Printed in Canada

FAMILY, WELFARE, AND THE STATE

Between Progressivism and the New Deal

Mariarosa Dalla Costa
Translated by Rafaella Capanna

Brooklyn, NY

TO MY FATHER FRANCESCO
AND MY MOTHER MARIA GHIDELLI

CONTENTS

ABBREVIATIONS

AAA	Agricultural Adjustment Administration
ADC	Aid to Dependent Children
AFL	American Federation of Labor
AJS	*American Journal of Sociology*
BPW	Board of Public Welfare
CCC	Civilian Conservation Corps
CIO	Committee of Industrial Organization (Since 1938: Congress of Industrial Organization)
CWA	Civil Works Administration
FDD	Five-Dollar Day
FERA	Federal Emergency Relief Act / Administration
FSA	Farm Security Administration
IWW	Industrial Workers of the World
HOLC	Home Owners' Loan Corporation
NAM	The National Association of Manufacturers
NIRA	National Industrial Recovery Act
PWA	Public Works Administration
RFC	Reconstruction Finance Corporation
RPAA	Regional Planning Association of America
SSA	Social Security Act
TVA	Tennessee Valley Authority
UNIA	Universal Negro Improvement Association
USA	United States of America
WPA	Works Progress Administration
WTUL	Women's Trade Union League
YWCA	Young Women's Christian Association

FOREWORD TO THE NEW EDITION

By Liz Mason-Deese

Originally published in Italian in 1983, at a time when the capitalist system was undergoing profound transformations, *Family, Welfare, and the State* continues to provide crucial insights for feminist and workers' struggles today. The COVID-19 pandemic and corresponding economic, social, and political crises rendered visible another long-standing crisis: the crisis of care. Capital and the state seek to push responsibility for managing this crisis into the household, that domestic space, and onto women's shoulders. Suddenly, women were simultaneously responsible not only for our own paid employment (when we have it!) and our usual burden of domestic work, but also educating and caring for children who were home all day, other sick and elderly family members who lost access to care, and extra cleaning and enforcement of health protocols to keep the virus at bay. As if this were not enough, women were often on the "front lines" carrying out "essential work," often without appropriate safety precautions, thereby putting themselves and the people they live with at risk.

Dalla Costa's methodological insights foreground the *construction* of the family and the domestic sphere, through specific state policies, emphasizing that there is nothing natural about women's role in the domestic space. It was in a specific historical context and to address specific needs of capital, that women, racialized differently, were pushed into the role of reproducing the workforce and managing the wage in its multiple dimensions. By not taking the domestic sphere and family for granted as the natural or necessary social unit, Dalla Costa renders visible a multiplicity of forms of resistance, of autonomous social reproduction and community care, that go beyond the family and enable the reproduction of something other than capitalist relations. Meanwhile, she shows how state intervention, through various welfare and social assistance programs, produced and solidified gendered familial roles, attempting to lock women into the role of reproducers of the workforce and managers of household consumption. This understanding of the role of welfare makes it impossible to have nostalgia for any type of Fordist or New Deal past and instead calls on us to invent and enact other futures. It is worth keeping these questions in mind as we confront the current restructuring of capital.

Today we are witnessing a global counteroffensive against the surging feminist tide of successive international feminist strikes and other mass mobilizations around the world. From restrictions on abortion rights in the United States and Poland, to campaigns against feminist sexual education (e.g., the Con mis hijos no se metas ("Don't mess with my children") campaign backed by the Church across Latin America), to the move for a return to "traditional families," this counteroffensive seeks to re-establish hierarchical and scripted gender roles. In line with Dalla Costa's analysis, this move is in direct response to women's organization and demands for more autonomy—whether in terms of an income, other forms of social assistance, or autonomous forms of social reproduction.

However, it is no longer primarily a matter of ensuring the reproduction of the male manufacturing worker. Now the household becomes a "laboratory for capital," as Lucía Cavallero and Verónica Gago have so succinctly put it, to ensure obedience through violence and debt.[1] Here, household debt operates as a mechanism to directly extract value from reproductive labor, whether through rent payments or debt incurred to pay utilities or food. This has reached unprecedented levels during COVID-

19, with its mandatory "stay at home" measures ensuring access to household income decreased at the same time expenses went up.

This new counteroffensive seeks to push responsibility for managing the crisis back into the domestic sphere in ever more insidious ways, both in economic and moral terms. Dalla Costa's analysis provides crucial insights for understanding the domestic space as both produced and productive. It is *produced* through state intervention in the form of welfare policies and their requirements and restrictions, through gendered labor market structures, through the lending policies of banks, etc. It is *productive* through (re)producing not only labor power in the form of male workers but also the wage relation itself in terms of hierarchies of obedience. Rather than a mere repetition of the past, however, today we are called upon to investigate precisely *how* the domestic sphere and gendered relations within it are being remade in response to the changing needs of capital. This inquiry will open new lines of struggle and enable the articulation of new alliances and demands.

Dalla Costa's perspective, while it highlights the ability of the state and capital to shape our most intimate spheres of life, is far from fatalistic. It shows how these interventions were a response to social mobilization and organization, and in turn, gave rise to new forms of resistance. From the mass movements of the unemployed to the everyday refusal of women across the country, Dalla Costa underscores how the pressure applied by social organization was what ultimately forced the state to take responsibility for social reproduction. In other words, welfare was fundamentally a response to social movements and organized communities, an acknowledgment of their demands, and an attempt to contain them. This response initiated a fundamental transformation in the relationship between the state, women, and the family.

Furthermore, by not taking the enclosed nuclear family as the norm, she also enables us to identify and recognize forms of resistance that might otherwise remain invisible. For example, she examines the racialized construction of the family in the United States and allows us to see how Black communities' reproduction beyond the nuclear family structure has often served as a form of survival and resistance to capitalist exploitation and racialized violence. This perspective also renders visible the multiple forms of autonomous social reproduction practiced in the United States during the New Deal era. While these autonomous practices have often been overlooked in favor of an emphasis on state policies, Dalla Costa shows how they were essential not only for survival but also for challenging established gender roles and positions, allowing women to exist beyond the patriarchy of the wage.

Mutual aid practices have long been central in marginalized communities—for example, drug users, AIDS patients, women seeking abortions—that are forcefully excluded from official forms of welfare and aid. With the COVID-19 pandemic, mutual aid practices have taken on an increasingly widespread and visible role. Faced with the lack of state support for those who needed all types of care during the pandemic, neighbors and community members came together to provide one another with food and medical supplies, and to arrange other care-giving services. In the rural New River Valley where I am writing from, a mutual aid network has provided thousands of food boxes, medical supplies, and other necessities for households across the valley. It has distributed food from a community garden, provided material support to a local anti-pipeline struggle, and managed to weave together relationships in a community suffering from multiple crises that extend well beyond the pandemic. This is only one example of the hundreds of similar mutual aid networks that have emerged or strengthened during the pandemic, and that far from being temporary measures, are proving to fundamentally transform community relations. One of the fundamental lessons we can draw from

Family, Welfare, and the State is that when we turn social reproduction over to the state, we allow the state to determine what is reproduced, and we take for granted that what we are reproducing will be capitalist social relations. When we take social reproduction into our own hands, when we recognize it as a terrain of struggle, we enable the production of *other social relations*.

In the context of the COVID-19 pandemic, as we attempt to articulate demands related to a feminist recovery, we must keep these lessons in mind. As the state and capital seek to push the management of the crisis into the household, we are called upon more than ever to challenge the naturalization of the domestic sphere and women's role in it. We can also ask what types of demands might be able to articulate the diverse segments of the working class, recognizing how the current crisis has affected us differently. What would calling for a mass income look like today? What have been the impacts of temporary pandemic relief measures, such as expanded unemployment benefits and eviction moratoriums? Can we defend these while ceding from the state's control of social reproduction? In other words, how can we call for collective responsibility of reproduction while maintaining our autonomy over those areas of our lives? What would it mean to challenge the domestication and individualization of responsibility for the pandemic, women's increasing workloads and moral responsibilities, and the nonrecognition of women as care providers? As we assume care for one another and the ecosystems we are enmeshed in, these are questions that must be addressed as a matter of collective responsibility to (re)produce different ways of living together.

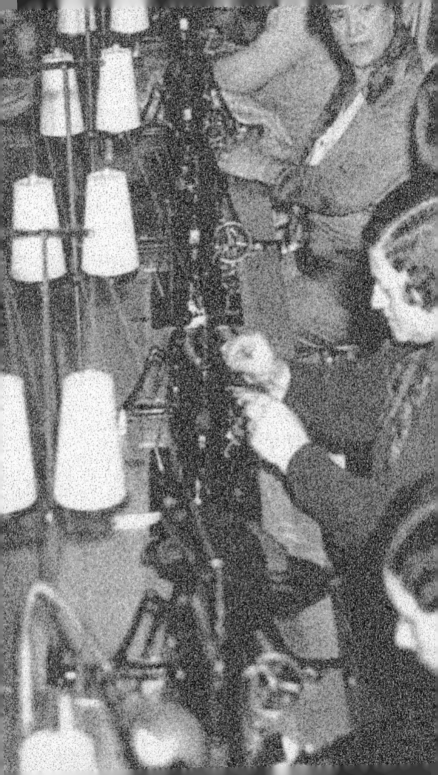

PREFACE

By Silvia Federici

As THE END OF THE WELFARE STATE is calling for a reassessment of the politics of the New Deal—its main point of origin in the United States—the publication of a U.S. edition of Mariarosa Dalla Costa's *Family, Welfare, and the State: Between Progressivism and the New Deal* could not be more timely.

Originally published in Italy in 1983, as the welfare state was already undergoing an historic crisis, the book centers on the new relation that the New Deal instituted between women and the state, and the development of a new reproductive regime in which the working-class housewife plays a strategic role as the producer of the workforce and manager of the worker's wage.

This is an aspect of New Deal politics that to this day remains understudied. It is crucial to an understanding of not only the limits of the welfare state, but also the paths to be taken in the construction of alternatives to it. Even the theorists of Italian *Operaismo*, who described the New Deal as a turning point in the management of class relations and as capital's first conscious integration of the class struggle in its development plans, have ignored the central relationship of women and the state underpinning this historic change in class relations. The New Deal, for Operaist political theorists like Mario Tronti, marked the institutionalization of collective bargaining and the transformation of the state into an agent of economic planning.[1] It was part of a Keynesian deal in which wage increases would be exchanged for and matched by labor productivity, with the state and the unions acting as guarantors of the equilibrium to be achieved.

What Dalla Costa shows, however, is that the complex social architecture upon which the New Deal relied was at all points dependent on a reorganization of the reproduction of the workforce and the integration of women's domestic labor and the family in the schemes of American capitalism. According to the New Dealers' plans, it was the woman's task to ensure that the higher family wage, which workers would gain through their newly acquired collective-bargaining power, would be productively expended and actually contribute to the production of a more disciplined, more pacified, and more productive workforce. As such, the "house-worker" was the strategic subject on which the success or failure of the New Deal depended, while essential to the exploitation of her work was the invisibilization of her labor.

Like many historians before her, Dalla Costa acknowledges that the New Deal continued trends that had been developing on both sides of the Atlantic since the last decades of the nineteenth century, culminating on the eve of WWI with Fordism. As she argues, there is no doubt, that the wage contract stipulated in the Ford factories in 1914—with its revolutionary introduction of the five-dollar-a-day wage and the reorganization of domestic life it promoted—was the model for the welfare and labor provisions of the New Deal. Fordism was the laboratory for the rationalization of domestic work that the New Deal required. In the Fordist "deal," the housewife was no longer expected to contribute to the production of consumption goods, which could now be produced industrially on a large scale, but to provide wise management of the wage and the socialization of the new generation—innovations that, in the Progressive Era, became the object of the new science of rationalization.

With the New Deal, for the first time, the state assumed the responsibility for the social reproduction of the worker, not only through the introduction of collective bargaining, but also through the institutionalization of housework—smuggled in, however, as "the work of love." As Dalla Costa shows, it was only with the New Deal that the state began to plan the "social factory"—

that is, the home, the family, the school, and above all women's labor—on which the productivity and pacification of industrial relations was made to rest.

Dalla Costa's guidance through these historic developments—with a narrative spanning from the Fordist era to the Great Depression and the enactment of the Social Security Act of 1935—and in particular, her analysis of the social forces these developments responded to, including their implications for worker-capital relations and for relations within the working class, is one the greatest merits of Dalla Costa's work. But there are many other aspects of the book that make it a major contribution to a feminist analysis of the New Deal, as well as a critical intervention advancing the ongoing debates on the role of the "public" and the construction of the "common."

First, Dalla Costa's reading precludes any celebratory interpretation of the New Deal as the "benign father" or "parental state" that some feminists in recent years have advocated. *Family, Welfare, and the State* leaves no doubt that the New Deal was not only the last resort to "save capitalism" from the danger of working-class revolution, and was in essence a productivity deal, it was also structured to maintain a patriarchal and racist order. Social Security was reserved for waged workers while domestic workers, even when working for pay, were excluded from it. Racial discrimination, exploitation, and domination too were pervasive in every aspect of its administration, from job creation to the disbursement of the only Social Security funds houseworkers would receive, namely Aid to Dependent Children (ADC, AFDC).[2] Dalla Costa nevertheless acknowledges the importance of this social security provision for women, as it opened a new terrain of confrontation with the state that in the 1960s was to assume mass proportions. This provision enabled women to achieve a degree of autonomy without relying on the male wage and inspired an international Wages for Housework Campaign of which Dalla Costa was one of the founders and main promoters.

An additional merit of Dalla Costa's work is that it highlights the prominent creative role that women played in both the social and factory struggles of the 1930s and its transformation of family relations. *Family, Welfare, and the State* brings attention to another important, but still ignored, aspect of the New Deal regarding the social context in which it was hatched. This is the great variety of initiatives that workers across the U.S. put in place to create autonomous forms of self-reproduction. To this day, little has been written about this impressive surge of self-organization, which reached proportions exceeding the experiments with self-management that we have witnessed in Argentina, with workers taking over factories to produce the necessities of life.[3] This is a history that today must be revisited as we ask whether our energies and our movements should concentrate on restoring or defending the welfare state, or constructing more autonomous forms of reproduction.

Were the New Deal and the institutions of the welfare state the saviors of the working class, or were they the destroyers of its self-reproducing capacities? As this question is presently coming to the center of radical political debate, at least in the U.S., an evaluation of the "reproductive" politics of the New Deal is more important than ever, and Dalla Costa's work is a powerful contribution to it.

Silvia Federici
Brooklyn, NY

INTRODUCTION

THIS BOOK IS INTENDED TO FILL A GAP in the literature on the New Deal concerning the relationship between women and the state, and therefore, the roles assumed by the family and women in President Franklin D. Roosevelt's plan. It is important to begin by precisely defining these themes to best bring into focus the relationship between the state and social reproduction in the U.S. in the 1930s.

Much has been written on the institution of collective bargaining as a new form of management for class relationships. Likewise, studies have been dedicated to the propulsive role of public spending for promoting development. It should also be shown how, through the policies of the New Deal, a vast and articulate operation directed at restructuring the reproduction of labor power came into being, and how the state's planning efforts intended to integrate this force with the modalities of development. Consequently, the new role assumed by public spending responded to the need for investment in human capital as a means of increasing the productivity of labor.

The New Deal provided answers to problems of labor reproduction that were already being addressed in the second half of the nineteenth century by technological innovations and during the prewar period by Fordism. These instances highlight the centrality of investment in human capital for the purpose of increasing labor productivity. One can easily observe the correlation between Marshall's recommendations (*Principles of Economics*, 1890) for investing in the working class and Ford's "five dollars a day" policy, as well as the criteria that inspired the Social Security Act of 1935. It took the struggles of the 1930s to *generalize awareness of the value of human resources* even though the most progressive exponents of capital had previously expressed this need.

The state's new role in relation to the economy— particularly its acceptance of the budget deficit and expansion of public spending to support demand—could function to propel development only if worker consumption passed through an arc of activities capable of guaranteeing the formation of a physically efficient and psychologically disciplined working class that, above all, was able to accept more intense work rhythms. All the initiatives in this direction revolved around strengthening the family—primarily through women's domestic work— because the income paid by the state, or wages, resulted in the greater productivity of labor power. Caring for children and a husband required a woman to know how to carry out a complex range of tasks which, until then, had not been required. Knowing how to prepare a balanced meal was just one of the most important material tasks of domestic work. In addition to the reproductive labor of housewives, the state began taking direct responsibility for reproducing and improving labor power. To give one example, programs offering free lunches in schools responded to the concern of establishing a level of physical efficiency in the new generations to overcome the impasse of the Depression generation as quickly as possible. The attention that the social sciences increasingly devoted to issues such as the home, diet, sexuality, birthrates, health, education, and leisure always led to this central need for an adequate science of reproductive and social planning. Another aspect of state intervention concerned the function of social assistance. This did not just mean improving the level of physical reintegration of labor power, but rather insuring its subsistence independently of both perturbations induced by the production cycle on employment opportunities and the subjective capability (disability, seniority) of the person to be employed. This system of measures was intended to produce a new economic and social order. The unfolding of these new social features, however, presupposed the centrality of the family and the work of women within it.

We can therefore say that, if the New Deal represented the first comprehensive agreement between the state and the working class, in which the working class was guaranteed a certain level of reproductive security in exchange for an increase in labor productivity, the effectiveness of such a pact passed significantly through the restructuring of the family and the intensification of women's domestic work. Even the work of women outside the home, in the areas and in the percentages allowed, would contribute to the subsistence and cohesion of the family during the Depression.

The New Deal remained the model social pact for the entire postwar period up to Kennedy's New Frontier policy (which featured investment in mass university education with the aim of developing the scientific-technological potential of the nation after the event of the Soviets' Sputnik launch in 1957) and especially until Johnson's "War on Poverty" and "Great Society" policies were implemented after the 1960s race riots in the ghettos.

The 1970s witnessed the historic end of the New Deal in the U.S., and of similar development plans in the countries it had inspired. In the name of fighting inflation, stagnation of economic development, and the erosion of profits, the Reagan administration passed a series of measures that seemed to turn back the clock to the time of Hoover. The dismantling of public spending on social assistance brought about cuts to welfare, Medicaid, Medicare, school lunches, subsidies for low-income housing, and student loans. With the 1983 federal budget, this process has also begun to affect Social Security, the sacred cow of the New Deal. In the name of *laissez faire* and supply-side economics (meaning reduced public spending for social assistance but fewer taxes for industry in order to encourage investment), there is an attack on the main assumption of the New Deal that the state should take responsibility for social reproduction, thus denying that state intervention in reproduction results in an increase in labor productivity. Though never explicitly stated, this is the basic premise of Reagan's policy of implementing widespread cuts in welfare.

The popular slogans of the 1980s are modeled on liberal-Hooverian themes: "we need to encourage private charity"; "the jobs are there, you just have to look for them"; "if people are unemployed it's because they refuse to adapt to low wages." Is it a return to Hoover? No, even if the current economic situation resembles that of the Great Depression, with thirteen million unemployed and a general condition of rampant poverty.

The Reagan administration's strategy of reducing public expenditure on social assistance while increasing spending on weapons is not a contingency policy, but the expression of a historical turning point in the relationship between capital and the working class—that is, in the form of accumulation and the agreement which lies at its foundation. This policy is accompanied by a massive industrial restructuring aimed at dismantling the type of political recomposition that came about during the 1960s through welfare struggles. The struggles of mothers on welfare have played an important role in this regard, acting as an indicator of the overall struggles of the women's movement against a mode of social reproduction undergirded by free domestic labor and subordination. Behind the wage claims, reflected in political pressure in the area of welfare and on the labor market, there was a withdrawal of women from free labor and the regimentation of the family, and with it the undermining of that entity as a means and guarantee of the productive result of investments in the area of reproduction. Since the mid-1970s, widespread worker disaffection—e.g., absenteeism at work, the tendency for workers to retire earlier, to cycle through jobs—has been discussed by economists as the "feminization" of male workers' behavior. The social struggles of women on the terrain of reproduction in the '60s and '70s have certainly been an important factor in breaking the balance between production and reproduction on which the Keynesian plan was founded. The continuous increase of female-headed households, the concurrent increase of divorces, and the sudden population decline during the 1970s, are only several of the most immediately obvious indicators of the limits of the presuppositions on which the cycle of postwar development was founded.

We have now come to a general recognition in political and economic areas that the forms of "social security" created by the New Deal are responsible for a set of expectations that is no longer compatible with the productivity and competitiveness of American capital. Indeed, the industrial restructuring that the Reagan administration has put into action has faced no real obstacles. At its center lies the end of mass industrial production, and with it, the end of a certain kind of working class, enabled by a certain kind of wage structure. The sectors of economic development that have been the strongest since the postwar period (auto, steel, rubber, construction), and which were producers not only of mass goods but also of more homogeneous mass wages, are experiencing a historical decline that verges on crisis. These manufacturing sectors are being replaced by a pyramidal production and wage system. At the top of this new system are the high-tech sectors: energy, computer science, and biogenetics. At the bottom is the magnum sea of the service sector, in which *reproduction services* have become a large part (food services, healthcare, etc.). Many areas of domestic work are moved out of the house and reorganized into waged positions. There is also a vast "industrial black market," in industries ranging from textiles to electronics, maintained by the labor of migrant workers and women.

Cuts to public spending on reproduction, the programmed *absenteeism* of the state with respect to planning in this area, and industrial restructuring are all closely linked. Reproduction, so to speak, is left to "free initiative" in the sense that everyone is empowered individually outside of a social plan. Despite Reagan's rhetoric on the importance of family, there is no family policy. The *housing crisis*, and the building crisis more generally, are signs of this. Today, we take for granted that the American dream—that is, having one's own home—is no longer possible for most people. What we are seeing is a real attack on *state investment in working-class reproduction*. Mass unemployment is the prerequisite for a compression of the expectations of women and men forced into fierce competition in the labor market. Meanwhile, the deindustrialization of the United States, advocated by the liberal-democratic wing of the American Establishment (the left, trade unions, certain sections of the Democratic Party), does not really seem to be able to offer any capitalist alternative to the mass devaluation of the working class. Indeed, the new wage structure not only produces much deeper differences and hierarchies within the working class but also foresees a general lowering of the standard of living.

ONE

MASS PRODUCTION AND THE NEW URBAN FAMILY ORDER

THE CRISIS OF 1929 SIGNALLED, for the first time in U.S. history, a breakdown in the relationship between employment and unemployment. This breakdown, however, would not seem definitive to American capitalists, or to the Rooseveltian state that would march into war with the illusion of a lasting solution to the problem of employment. But except for the absorption that took place during the war, unemployment would prove to be an endemic fact in the U.S. economy.

With the sudden explosion of mass unemployment in 1929, the reproduction of labor power also went into crisis, and therefore, so did the "generality" of family structure that was attained for the first time in 1914 with Henry Ford's landmark "Five-Dollar Day" (FDD) strategy.[1] By instituting a policy in his factories, which has since become a famous argument for efficiency management, Ford indirectly defined the quantity and quality of domestic work necessary to sustain the productivity of factory labor.

Between 1914 and 1924, the state significantly curbed immigration, primarily as a reactionary response to workers' struggles that developed in the first decade of the century and to the militant activity of the Industrial Workers of the World (IWW).[2] This forestalled the possibility of the aggressive encouragement of immigration that had characterized the previous period of productive development. Increasingly, the quantitative and qualitative reproduction of labor power would become a problem that would have to be solved internally.

The shift in perspective on wages reflected by Ford's policy reveals a certain awareness of the necessity of providing reproductive support to workers in the most rationalized sectors. That is, to working-class families dependent upon, on the one hand, the man's ability to earn a wage capable of supporting a wife and a home,[3] and on the other, the working-class housewife whose job must become, more and more exclusively, the production and reproduction of labor power.[4]

It is important to emphasize that not only did the level of the new wage implemented by Ford express a capitalist response to the costs of reproducing labor power,[5] but this increase was accompanied by an apparatus of control over family management, and thus over reproduction itself. The Five-Dollar Day—which *wasn't* paid to workers who had been on the job for less than six months, or to young people under twenty-one years of age, or to women—was still portrayed as a "benefit" one might not qualify for or which could be taken away if one didn't lead a "moral" or hygienic life. The wage could be withheld or revoked, for example, if one kept bad company, had family quarrels, faced an imminent divorce or had already filed for one, or if one was prone to gambling, the use of tobacco, alcohol, etc. As H. Beynon notes, this era marked the beginning of cooperation between university-trained experts (sociologists, psychologists, psychotechnicians) and employers.[6] Ford used a "sociology department" and a corps of inspectors and controllers whose task was to enter the homes of workers, investigate their lives, and *how they spent their pay*. The "benefit" of the FDD could, in fact, be denied to any workers whose conduct was such that this wage level was deemed a handicap rather than an incentive for moral rectitude.[7]

Women were not amongst the beneficiaries of the FDD because according to Ford's declared hopes, they should get married. The Fordian wage was supposed to be managed by the housewife, who would be relieved by the industrial production of necessary goods (i.e., necessary for the reconstitution of the labor force) of the many old tasks that previously burdened her. Now these goods were available for purchase in the form of commodities. Therefore, they would no longer be acquired through a woman's ability to supply them directly, but rather through her ability to manage wages.[8]

In the overall effort of rationalization that characterized the beginning of the century, the revaluation of the housewife, and more specifically, the redefinition of her duties, met the need to re-establish the institution of the family which had been greatly weakened as an agent of social reproduction in the previous century.[9] The beginning of the twentieth century marked the discovery of domestic work *as work*, but much of the feminist movement was co-opted by the forces that drove the moral valorization of housework. "The Movement for Domestic Science" reflects the intersection of feminism and reformism. In correspondence with rationalization in the factory, the rationalization of domestic work—that is, of the process of reproduction of labor power—sought maximum results with minimum expenditure.

In the attempt to Americanize immigrant communities, this directive would be given to women by social workers and a method of control of workers' wages would be directly established.[10] These efforts would not be put into effect everywhere in the same way however. Ford, hoping that compulsive Americanization would bring about a more immediate productivity of the worker at the factory, interpreted Americanization more brutally and, hence, with shorter breadth. The International Institute was established in 1911 as a division of the YWCA to assist immigrant women. Together with social workers, local chapters of the International Institute developed programs dedicated to the recovery of community, a central theme in the social sciences and in the social progressivism of the Protestant tradition. In this way, they were able to facilitate a less violent, and therefore more reliable, cultural incorporation of immigrants into American society.[11] Overall, one can see how an invitation to the scientific management of domestic work in the first two decades of the century largely constituted an invitation to *parsimony*. In 1912, Wesley C. Mitchell, a leading academic who became economic adviser to Roosevelt, wrote:

> ... So long as the family remains the most important unit for spending money, so long will the art of spending lag behind the art of making money. ... The young wife seldom approaches her housework in a professional spirit. She holds her highest duty that of being a good wife and a good mother. Doubtless to be a good manager is part of this duty; but the human part of her relationship to husband and children ranks higher than the business part. ... She cannot divide her duties as a human being so sharply from her duties as a worker. Consequently, her housekeeping does not assume objective independence in her thinking, as an occupation in which she must become proficient.[12]

In agreement with other economists of the time, Mitchell considers with satisfaction the trap in which women were caged. The wife's primary incentive to work was the "human relationship" she had with her family members. Meanwhile, since the beginning of the century, certain feminists had already raised the question of the possibility for women to live independently, without a husband.[13] That is, with autonomous sexual choices, living in their own homes, and refusing to sacrifice themselves for their children.[14] They also raised the issue, albeit sporadically, of retribution for domestic labor—either as a share of the husband's wages or as direct provision by the state.[15]

The issue, however, could not have been isolated if the socialist newspaper *Chicago Evening World* hadn't printed (also in 1912) an article which emphasized this new quality of the women's struggle:

> Women who are housewives are not paid wages directly from a capitalist boss; consequently they do not always

see their connection with the economic system. It is a bit indirect, but nevertheless it is a close connection. When a boss buys the labor power of a worker, he also buys the labor power of his wife. The harder the work that man is asked to carry out, the more that is required from his wife. A worker who gets up early to have breakfast with the light on and goes out to the factory or mine for the whole day could not perform his duties if it were not for the faithful, personal service and care of the woman who keeps his house. She gets up in the early hours to make his breakfast, packs his lunch box and puts all the prepared things in his hands. His time must be spared, his energy saved. Both belong to the boss. She must consume herself to save him. . . . Women who have received a salary were the first among the female sex to awaken to the realization of their political and economic necessity, since their connection with the capitalist structure of society was direct and evident. The housewives are waking up more slowly, but they are awakening. They begin to see that the capitalist boss of the mine or factory actually controls the labor power of women in the home, taking hold of her life day by day, without pay or recognition.[16]

During this time the state developed massive social reforms. With the concession of the need for investment in human capital, the state focused its reformation activity above all on women and children. With regard to education, there were initiatives that focused on countering the disintegration of human relationships, especially noticeable in rapidly expanding urban areas. A general lamentation was the fact that the family and the church no longer functioned as they had before, so the school was looked to as the new primary site for socialization and education. In 1902, John Dewey took the idea of the social center to the conference of the National Education Association, where he argued that schools should be "means for bringing people and their ideas and beliefs together, in such ways as will lessen friction and instability, and introduce deeper sympathy and wider understanding."[17] He thought that the use of schools as social centers would improve the quality of life in cities, providing recreational alternatives to the brothels, saloons, and dance halls.[18] Education thus became a fundamental sociopolitical sector of American life.

As for women, their work and the family, state intervention was widespread. The Department of Agriculture, together with the Home Economics Association, sent thousands of women, with or without pay, to teach other women the basics of modern domestic efficiency. Recalling how the Movement for Domestic Science and its introduction in schools had a counterpart in Germany in the 1920s, G. Bock and B. Duden stress how the Smith-Lever and Smith-Hughes Acts constituted milestones in the history of the Movement for Domestic Science since they cemented a permanent relationship between the movement itself and the federal government.[19] For example, legislation was developed with regard to the control of food.[20] Directives were given on health, hygiene, education, and good family order. Measures were also taken in the field of welfare. For the first time, a system of family allowances and tax differentiation in relation to marital status and family was promoted.

The state was no longer just a legislator but also an *administrator*, even if social planning essentially remained utopian.[21] It would only be with the New Deal, and with attempts to plan class dynamics, that the problem would truly be addressed. Hitherto, planning was carried out within a limited social framework, and with the same capitalist awareness that viewed the social framework as totally extraneous to the sphere of production. The state's new role as arbiter of social relations was soon accepted, but not without resistance. By the early 1920s the movement for the Americanization of immigrants ended. Direct repression and the hunt for red subversives (the Red Scare of 1919–1920) expressed the new attitude of capital.[22] Its reaction in the 1920s, from factory repression to social moralization, was entirely aimed at the establishment of a new "work ethic":

> *The highest type of laborer is the man who holds a steady job.*
> He is part of an industry; he has an occupation. He
> is a citizen in a community; generally the father of a
> family; probably a member of one or more lodges,
> and very frequently of a church.[23]

It is significant that in this period, the Young Women's
Christian Association's (YWCA) International Institutes
polarized their activity with respect to second-generation
women and promoted initiatives aimed at their socialization. If women's management of wages and the home
remained a constant topic of discussion, a change of inter-
locutors and the mode of action could be sensed. Now, one
looked to the daughters of immigrants. On the one hand
it meant taking action to make the generational contrast
between immigrant parents and children less disruptive,
and on the other, it meant pursuing a nonconflictual emergence of the new figure of the American daughter, wife,
and mother. At a convention of the International Institutes
in 1924, having to decide which field to work in for the
future, the majority of institutions opted for the problem of
second-generation girls. A commission was created for that
purpose in 1925, namely the Commission on the Study of
the Second Generation Girl, and in 1928 it changed its
name to the Commission on First Generation Americans.
The reason that led to the change was explained as the
following: when you say *second generation* you think of the
past. When you say *first-generation Americans*, you think about
the future.[24]

As for the social sciences, from 1905 to 1909 the
American Journal of Sociology saw a rise in the percentage of
population studies (on immigration) to the level of nine
percent compared to one percent for the period 1900 to
1904. With the outbreak of the war in Europe, American
sociologists focused their discussions on the need to control immigration. Mostly based on criteria put forward
as scientific, they denied the possibility that immigrants
from Southern and Eastern Europe could be assimilated,

and pressed for the urgent restriction of immigration. This is especially true of the time of the United States' entry into the conflict, as is evident in the *AJS*, which officially defined what sociology was. The other fact which was emphasized was the absolute exclusion from the journal of socialist- or radical-inspired materials which, however, found hospitality in other large-circulation journals and newspapers.[25]

The family ideology was arguably perfected in the 1920s. The affectionate and "disinterested" nature of women, along with their unpaid work, was increasingly and subtly put in opposition to the cooperative nature of work in a factory, labor that accumulated and took advantage of social knowledge and loaded itself with potential for revolt.

Whereas in the years before World War I the middle-class housewife could usually count on the cooperation of housekeepers and relatives, afterwards it became increasingly difficult to find women willing to perform waged domestic work.[26] Relatives and housekeepers looked instead to the new employment opportunities for women. World War I proved to be that watershed moment for the ideology and structure of the American family.[27] We can appreciate how before the war, at the level of the middle classes, when the housewife was essentially the administrator of the home, it was not difficult to propagate an ideology of domestic labor as real work. It was presumed that this labor wasn't burdensome, except possibly to a very limited extent. After the war, however, the same middle-class housewife got involved in the direct management of domestic work, given the growing absence of housekeepers. Administration and provision of that labor became a single entity.

For all of the 1920s, what was referred to as the "industrial revolution in the home" was far from lightening the load of tasks around which women's work was articulated. Yes, some technological innovations were introduced in the home and became increasingly widespread, such as electric lighting, electric irons, gas cookers and washing machines (though not yet with an automatic cycle). The bathroom mania which exploded in those years was certainly also in relation to the use of electricity for heating water and rooms. Equally, the use of electricity in refrigeration, especially in railway cars that transported goods, allowed noteworthy amounts of fresh products to enter the market, which enabled many women to set aside the job of preserving fruits and vegetables during the summer.[28] There was a growing spread of a series of products on the market that the new generation of housewives would have to get to know and learn to buy *for the first time*.[29] Meanwhile, the usual tasks of raising and caring for children and reproduction of the husband became more diverse and complex. The functions of socialization acquired an ever more important place in domestic work itself. Not only did each material task have to be weighed, planned, measured, and coordinated even more, but the overall set of duties—both material and immaterial—in which domestic work was structured further widened.[30] All this constituted a new workload which would have to be carried out by women without pay.

Consequently, there was a decisive turning point in the ideology of the family. It emphasized domestic work as a labor of love and, correspondingly, stigmatized its transgression as a fault.[31] Even advertising targeted at women was polarized in this way.[32] Cleaning perfectly to destroy the very last germ is not work but a way to cherish loved ones. Not doing so is being a bad wife and a bad mother.[33]

Paradoxically, while a series of important technological innovations were implemented in the home, as we have just seen, the social sciences diminuitized the importance of technological rationalization at the domestic level compared to previous years. These centered the subject entirely on the woman's role—her capacity for dedication and sacrifice.

While the number of children that women had to care for continued to decline (with a particularly sharp

15

pace in the decades from 1920 to 1940), social psychology prescribed the devotion of a new attention to children and adolescents, binding the mother to new modes of child-rearing which would often make her feel guilty for having to contravene them and for not considering herself competent enough.[34] In 1928, John B. Watson, the founder of the behaviorist school of psychology in the United States, published his *Psychological Care of Infant and Child* in which he intended to persuade mothers of the seriousness of their task. This book exerted considerable influence. In correspondence with the new commitment expected from parents, training courses for parents were instituted and directed particularly at mothers. Here we must emphasize that the work commitments of many American women in those years were complicated by the fact that they came from rural areas. In fact, at that time there was a mass exodus from the countryside to the cities. Consequently, women who came to live in towns faced not only the challenge of having to manage the home in a totally different environment, but also one that demanded a much higher standard of family life, and thus a much higher level of consumption was required.[35]

Therefore, these were the first women responsible for the new way of functioning required of families—both in terms of consumption and of family values more generally—as a necessary guarantor for the adaptation of the whole society to the new productive and political phase that opened up after the war. From this came the impetus for many women to take on an outside job. The famous theory of the "pin-money worker" (one who works for the superfluous), would immediately accompany their search for paid work as well as being the leitmotif in the Depression years when the needs of their family income would become even more stringent.[36]

What follows are some characteristics of female employment in the period we are considering. Only five percent of women employed due to the war had entered the labor market for the first time on that occasion. The others, for the most part, were transfers. And at the end of the war, the reverse substitution was just as fast. Women's employment, which had experienced a significant increase only in the first decade of the century, would continue to represent, from 1910 onwards, about one-fifth of total employment. In 1930, the number of employed women would be approximately 10.6 million compared to approximately 38 million men.

17

The most important aspect of women's employment from 1910 onwards was the percentage change in the individual sectors. In the white-collar sector, this percentage increased from 23.3 percent in 1910, to 38.5 percent in 1920, to 44.0 percent in 1930. In the field of personal and domestic services, it decreased from 31.3 percent in 1910, to 25.6 percent in 1920, and then rose to 29.6 percent in 1930. In the area designated as laborers and semiskilled operatives, this percentage decreased from 45.4 percent in 1910, to 35.8 percent in 1920, to 26.5 percent in 1930. The years from 1910 to the Great Crisis delineated new profiles of female employment, with the white-collar sector emerging more markedly in 1940.

The other peculiar aspect of women's employment during this period concerns that of married women. The percentage of employed married women, calculated in relation to the female population, experienced a significant increase from 1900 to 1910, rising from 5.6 percent to 10.7 percent, but fluctuating a little before the Great Depression. It would drop to 9.0 percent in 1920 to climb to 11.7 percent in 1930. With regard to these women, from 1910 to 1920, one notes not so much an increase in the percentage employed, rather the fact that employment expanded greatly in the white-collar sector, from 21.5 percent in 1920 to 32.5 percent in 1930, whereas in previous years, expansion was mostly concentrated in the more unskilled areas.[37]

There are a few more details still to mention with regard to women's employment. During the 1920s, compared to the previous decade characterized by strong industrial expansion, female workers had to fall back on defensive struggles to maintain their jobs and their earlier political victories.[38] From 1910 to 1920 this front saw aggressive struggles that achieved some notable successes both in traditionally progressive states (New York, Massachusetts) and in the South. In the same period, there developed a series of federal and state investigations on the excessive length of the workday of children and women, and especially with regard to night work. But in the 1920s, while it can be assumed that a small proportion of women had now irreversibly entered the labor market, and that capitalist restructuring tended to maintain female employment at the compressed levels given, state focus was leaning rather toward the strengthening of the family.

State interest in strengthening the domestic role of women, and motherhood in particular, by providing financial support in the absence of male wages was significant. This interest was developed by individual states with efforts such as legislation on mothers' pensions. This legislation began in 1910 and extended to all but four states by 1930.

This legislation was aimed primarily at insuring the children of "deserving widows" but in some cases its application was extended to include the children of women who had been abandoned or divorced by their husbands, or whose husbands were in prison, hospitalized for mental illness, or permanently disabled. The movement for mothers' pensions was supported by women's organizations, and also by the courts that dealt with juvenile delinquency and noted the high percentage of children of single mothers among the cases submitted. Even at that time, the development of legislation on mothers' pensions was considered a phenomenon which more than any other testified to the "irresistible development of social insurance principles in the United States"—even though it was influenced by "moral and economic considerations" rather than by insurance criteria.[39] The problem increasingly tended to be

inscribed in a definition of poverty as a widespread phenomenon that could not be entrusted to voluntary charity.

In the spirit of "justice" and "democracy" that ani-
mated reformers, one could feel the urgency of making
the transition from private charity to responsibility of the
individual state, or even, as some demanded, the federal
government. In correspondence with the awareness of
the "environmental" origins of poverty, many felt that in
order to face the problem it was necessary to mobilize the
financial, organizational, and intellectual potential of the
community that only state administrations, and not volunteer agencies, could have. The mothers' pensions were
born together with the Board of Public Welfare (BPW),
which tried to discredit the philanthropic practices of
volunteer agencies and which redefined governmental
welfare functions in an urban-industrial context.[40] There
were two pivotal principles around which the debate on
the mothers' pensions grew: (1) the individualization of
assistance, and (2) the superiority of home life. This superiority was seen as providing an advantage economically
as well as in the quality of child-rearing.

In 1909, at the Conference on the Care of Dependent
Children, a principle that would become the cornerstone
of welfare policy in this field was formulated: "Home life
is the highest and finest product of civilization. Children
should not be deprived of it except for urgent and com-
pelling reasons."[41] President Theodore Roosevelt agreed
that "poverty alone should not disrupt the home."[42]
Therefore, during the Conference on the Care of
Dependent Children, a series of directives were formulated so that in cases where it was not possible to keep
the natural mother and child together, one got as close as
possible to a similar relationship. For example, adoption
was suggested whenever practicable, and where recourse
to public institutions was necessary, the construction of
"cottage units" was recommended, with no more than
twenty-five children per assistant so as to safeguard the
possibility of interindividual attention.

19

Again, I assert that the family remained *the* fundamental social institution. Nevertheless, the awareness that the new conditions of life related to industrialization and the urban context, to the extent that they often took away the family's ability to meet individual needs, started to make inroads in the political establishment. Accordingly, the state increasingly sought to carry out projects toward integrating family income. The legislation of mothers' pensions can be considered a very significant step with regard to the enactment of the Federal Maternity Law in 1921 which, G. Bock and B. Duden observe, may hardly be considered less significant than women's suffrage in 1920.[43]

In the era of mass production—not just in the material sense but also its reproduction on a psychic level, including its discipline and socialization—in which the correlate production of a new labor power required a specific relationship between the family and the labor market, the state needed to both regulate the labor market and strengthen the family. Its new interest and activity with regard to the mother, the family, childhood, and educational institutions foreshadowed the imminence of the passage from "residual" to planned intervention in the area of social assistance. That meant that the new profile of the welfare state could be defined only in carrying out the state role of planner that would recompose and refound, in a different relation, the production of commodities and the production and reproduction of labor power. This would redefine the relationship between the centrality of the family and above all the woman in it, the labor market, and the state.

TWO

THE CRISIS OF 1929 AND THE DISRUPTION OF THE FAMILY

THE CRISIS

Before discussing the economic framework of the period immediately preceding the crisis, some aspects of 1929 should be clarified straight away. The crisis, as Mauro Gobbini points out, was a "crisis of production, not over-production, and arises from the fact that while the factory system of mass production is universally extended, consumption is constrained by a distribution of income that still rewards the rentier and the stock market speculator." He continues:

> Economic activity is still dependent on guidelines that do not capture the novelty of the world market situation, the definitive triumph of industrial production and the international division of labor that this has imposed with respect to any other productive and organizational structure.[1]

In 1932 it was estimated that there were already 13 million unemployed. By 1933, there were 15 million Americans without jobs.[2] But it is good to pause, just to clarify the depth of the problem that arose. Unemployment was considered:

> "a global problem," not so much for the size it reached, but because of the contradictions expressed, for the danger represented in relation to an evolution of the factory system, which is not based on the professional stratification of labor, on the division between skilled

labor and unskilled labor, but on the expansion of the productive basis to which a constant level of profit does not correspond.[3]

In 1926, the Ford Company declared that 43 percent of the 7,782 different tasks carried out in its factories demanded just one day of training; 36 percent required from one day to a week of training; six percent from one to three weeks, and only 15 percent a longer period of time. According to these numbers, it was estimated that 85 percent of Ford workers could reach their full capacity in less than two weeks.[4]

Between 1922 and 1929, the national income grew from approximately $60 billion to about $87 billion and, by the end of spring to early summer of 1929, the index of industrial production reached its peak of 126.[5] Productivity was up 43.7 percent while the comparative cost per unit of labor had gone down. During the same years the mass wages of the workers in big business had increased by 30 percent while profit in relation to large corporations had risen by 76 percent. At the same time, income was dangerously concentrated, irrationally so, in relation to the development needs of the system. "By 1929, the 2.3 per cent of the population with incomes over $10,000 were responsible for two-thirds of the 15 billion dollars of savings."[6] While some sectors of big business had embarked on the path already indicated by Ford, of providing wages high enough to support a family, the rest of the population had a very low standard of living. Just before the crisis, 59 percent of the population still had an income of less than $2,000 a year.

Immediately after the war, the agricultural sector, which had developed in the war years, driven by a high demand and with remunerative prices, began to suffer a decline in demand given the ongoing decline in prices. From 1919 to 1921, the gross agricultural income fell from 17.7 billion to 10.5 billion. In the same period there was a fall in the agricultural price index from 215 to 124. Just as precipitously, land prices fell everywhere, while the burden of both taxes and debts increased. From 1916 to 1923, interest per acre more than doubled in cost.[7] Between 1919 and 1929, agricultural income fell, compared to the national income, from 22.9 percent to 12.7 percent. Millions of farmers had to abandon the countryside for the city. The rigidity of agricultural demand, resulting from the fact that the goods produced by agriculture could be purchased even on a subsistence wage, made raising the level of wages unnecessary. This was accompanied by stagnant population growth due to the cessation of large influxes of immigrants and the fact that after the war, Europe had begun to develop its own agriculture thus requiring fewer American products.

Even traditionally strong sectors such as mining and textiles registered a moment of great impasse during that period and the workers, both men and women, had already suffered several wage cuts. By 1930, the United Mine Workers were in a precarious situation. The coal industry was struggling in a highly anarchic competition finding itself at the same time with "too many mines and too many miners." On the one hand, the employers had failed to organize themselves, and on the other, "the workers' federation had not been able to penetrate several important industrial sectors, while the control of the sectors they at one time organized was slipping further and further away."[8]

In March 1924, the United Mine Workers and the owners of the mines of the North signed "an agreement under which the relatively high wages of the war period were maintained. But the introduction of mechanization in the unorganized mines of West Virginia and the opening of new mines in the South, allowing the exploitation of cheap labor, made the situation for the owners who had signed the agreement of 1924 intolerable. The result was a general reduction of wages and a steady decline of membership in the federation, which went from 600,000 to 150,000 members."[9]

23

As for the textile sector, limits on working hours and wages, layoffs, and consequent evictions for those who lived in the homes of the company were all part of the daily grind for the working adults, girls, and boys employed during the 1920s. Without the power to strongly negotiate the question of hours and wages, in a period when the battle on these issues was carrying on from state to state, with frequent court decisions that denied positive results even in the few states which got favorable rulings, it was the manufacturing working class that would bear the brunt of the crisis most severely.[10]

The political tradition of the IWW, which had involved struggles in the textile sector (as in Lawrence, Massachusetts in 1912), was over. The great steel strike of 1919 ended this period.[11] After that defeat, a more rationalized industry facilitated a fair degree of social harmony.

At the vanguard of the 1920s were the sectors of steel, automobiles, electrical equipment, oil and chemical products that developed in the northern states, and which also provided rising wages. In contrast, the South (with the exception of Birmingham and Montgomery, Alabama where steel was produced), continued to be characterized by agriculture and industries with low levels of capitalization and low wages, primarily textile and furniture factories.

It was in these areas that struggles broke out again, to resist the intensification of work rhythms, the worsening of working conditions, and the attempt to lower wages.[12] The efforts of the Women's Trade Union League (WTUL), for example, were aimed at supporting the workers of the clothing industry and helping maids and female workers in laundries, hotels, and beauty salons, to get away from positions with unlimited time obligations and paltry wages.[13] However, the WTUL could do very little due to the continued lack of support from the union, while the owners could still count on both macroscopic fractures of power within the working class and the arrogance of the judiciary, which was always ready to suppress demands for limits on working hours and the establishment of a minimum wage, dismissing them as the will of communism or socialism.[14] The domain of piecework at home, the subject of specific investigations by the WTUL, was obviously without any form of regulation. This field was fairly widespread and followed trends in employment.[15] That is, it expanded in times of industrial development and was reduced in times of recession. The areas affected were mainly those of clothing, embroidery, artificial flowers, knitting, food, tobacco, toys, and jewelry manufacturing.[16] In addition to women, children were employed, in violation of any law on child labor, sometimes working from the age of four.[17]

The efforts of the League, which almost always moved with the help of the Consumers' Leagues and the YWCA, would fail in the period preceding the Great Depression to save women in the weaker sectors from the total will of their bosses with regard to working hours, wages, safety, and overall conditions in the workplace, as well as on the level of employment itself.[18]

A boss's will was well supported by a judiciary apparatus that was fiercely hostile to any regulation in this area. With regard to women's employment, this attitude was a direct expression of a state that responded to women's problems at the time by simply ignoring them or saying that it wished there weren't any employed outside the home. In 1922, James L. Davis, Secretary of Labor said, "Women have a higher duty in a higher sphere of life. Eve was the companion and helpmate of Adam and his social equal in every sense, but it was up to Adam to protect Eve and to provide for her for the future. Personally I prefer to see a woman guide the destiny of a nation at home."[19]

At the same time, this state would find itself totally unprepared to deal with the problems of social disruption that the crisis would impose. First it had to understand the nature of the phenomenon that would explode and then the issues that would arise with it. With the kind of family that the most advanced, and rationalized, part of capital had structured, it acquired a formidable cell of

25

organization and social order. But with the crisis and its widespread lack of income, this family was undermined. The social order had been disrupted and the state would be called upon to rebuild it, this time having to act directly. The horror of the "Communist monster," having spread quickly after 1917, had frozen the capacity to think beyond the myth of "individualism at all costs" so entrenched in the capitalist consciousness.[20] The Hoover line of response to the crisis went from minimizing the problem, to urging people to "spread the work" (while at the same time not providing adequate support to realize this suggestion), to blocking the more urgent measures such as several Public Works projects presented to Congress in 1930, to directly shooting at demonstrators.[21]

Unemployment lines swelled visibly in the streets: from 429,000 in October of 1929, to 4,065,000 in January 1930, 8,000,000 in January 1931, and 9,000,000 in October of 1931.[22] The president deemed that these numbers were not yet sufficient to justify large-scale measures. From 1929 to 1932 the crisis pressed on, resulting in a collapse of industrial production by 50 percent. About 6,000 banks went under. Farm income went down by about 50 percent while industrial wages fell by about 45 percent. Not only were wage laborers and agricultural workers thrown into ruin but so too were the masses of the petty-bourgeois.[23] In an attempt to maintain prices, large quantities of agricultural products in the country were destroyed and industrial capacity was drastically reduced.[24] Unemployed people and their families struggled every day against hunger, became chronically ill, ransacked garbage to find food, were evicted from their homes, and roamed without money from one state to another in search of seasonal work.[25] Basically, along with unemployment began a massive process of family and social disruption which Hoover was still not able to recognize, and therefore did not deal with. Home and family, once guaranteed by men's wages, fell apart under the pressure of the crisis.

Other aspects of this period must be specified. The family that was most affected at a mass level was the white family. Black workers, who resisted and fought against threats of discrimination and dismissal in the recessions of the 1920s, but who were still a minority in the industry, faced the most discrimination proportionally, in terms of job losses.[26] Yet it was the white family that the state and capital strained to rebuild, because it was this family and not the Black family (or rather, Black community) which at a mass level was assigned the task of sustaining working-class production, and of representing either order or disorder at a social level.

Black workers were also heavily discriminated against by the various aid and work plans because they were considered overabundant in relation to the need for their integration into industry, and because, from capital's perspective, they represented the weakest point in the labor market that could be abandoned to itself. On the other hand, mass migration to the North had not yet begun, though it became the norm in the 1940s and 1950s.[27] The Black community had not yet reached the level of power that it would attain in the 1960s. When Roosevelt posed the problem of ensuring a basic level of reproduction of labor power through welfare plans, the attitude towards Black people indicated that the state and capital did not care at all about Black labor power.

Of course women, too, were scarcely considered by labor plans. Because they had to return from the streets and casual jobs to domestic work, those who had outside employment could easily be discriminated against, even if the New Deal legislation devoted a few paragraphs to their minimum wage and work schedules.

THE DISRUPTION OF THE FAMILY

The vast amount of literature available in the 1930s on "family disruption" and "crime and its causes" is both an index of the problem and a major source of information.[28] Some "pathological causes" of delinquency, typical

27

of Cesare Lombroso's thought, still appear among the reasons cited to explain the occurrence of crime, but the literature is generally focused on "social causes" and is remarkably unanimous in identifying the "broken home" headed by only one parent as a major cause of crime.[29]

Broken or not, families by the millions were without a roof over their heads. So the resultant excessive overcrowding, and thus a lack of privacy within spaces set up as shelters, was frequently identified as a cause of crime.[30] Many people, unable to pay the rent, began to build shacks anywhere they could find unoccupied land:

> Along the railroad embankment, beside the garbage incinerator, in the city dumps, there appeared towns of tarpaper and tin, old packing boxes and old car bodies. Some shanties were neat and scrubbed; cleanliness at least was free; but others were squalid beyond belief, with the smell of decay and surrender. Symbols of the New Era, these communities quickly received their sardonic name: they were called Hoovervilles.[31]

But only the lucky could find refuge in Hoovervilles. Many families were completely torn apart: children were entrusted to friends or relatives who were still able to support them, husbands and wives were separated temporarily or permanently, each searching for their own survival. Men and women, young and old, were homeless, waiting in endless food lines, sleeping on the ground, traipsing from city to city in the hope of finding work.[32]

It is estimated that in 1932, a million and a half to two million people became vagrants and of these, two to three hundred thousand were young men, while 1 in 20 were women.[33] Often, older children would abandon home so that their younger siblings had enough to eat. With the pressures of the Depression, the number of women who migrated also increased. In 1933, the Women's Bureau deemed that there were ten thousand vagrant women in the country, but that this estimate corresponded to one-sixth of the total, and that in any case there had been an increase of ninety percent over the previous year.[34] The women whom the Women's Bureau was referring to were almost all under thirty; many held a degree but were jobless.

Married women tended to stay with their husbands and children when they could. Even in the veterans' camp in Washington, among the thousands of men were their wives and children. And this, despite the fact that the conditions of the camp offered only poor quality food, there were flies everywhere, diseases on the rise, and the smells of waste, sweat and urine all around "in the swampy land under the steaming sun."[35]

But the crisis broke families everywhere and discouraged the formation of new ones and new births. The decline of marriage can be seen in the decreasing marriage rate per thousand of the population, which went from 10.1 in 1929, to 9.2 in 1930, to 8.6 in 1931, to 7.9 in 1932.[36] Births, which had had a yearly average of 20 per thousand at the end of the 1920s, went down to an average of 18.9 in 1930, to 18 in 1931, to 17.4 in 1932, to 16.6 in 1933. In 1931, the total birth rate was 17 percent less than that of 1921, and 10 percent less than that of 1926.[37] Those who were born, observes Bernstein, would belong to the "Depression generation," and their relatively weak physical structure would make them unfit for entering the labor market.[38] Surveys taken in schools in 1931 showed that 85–90 percent or even 99 percent of children had a lower weight than normal and were therefore "drowsy and lethargic."[39]

Hoover, however, was of the opinion that there were at least ten million underdeveloped children and the Children's Bureau of the Labor Department estimated that in 1932 there were two hundred thousand boys who roamed the country in search of food.[40] In 1929, illegitimate births were 31 per thousand, a much higher figure than in previous years.[41] The number of abandoned people ("poor people's divorce") increased. Meanwhile, the number of legal divorces decreased because they were too expensive.[42] The number of suicides also increased. Death from starvation was a widespread fate. The famous 1931 study of New York hospitals, which reported about 100 cases of death by starvation, does not give an adequate idea of the magnitude of the phenomenon.[43] There was a chronic increase in communicable diseases such as tuberculosis, syphilis, and influenza. The number of patients in tuberculosis sanatoriums almost doubled. A study of the U.S. Public Health Service recorded that in the families of the unemployed, people got sick 66 percent more frequently than families of workers who had a job.[44]

With regard to men or women who went off alone, Bakke retorts, "In our society, the family, not the individual, is the economic unit."[45] Inevitably, even when the head of the family remained with his brood but was unemployed, a clear process of "denigration of the father" had begun. Again, Bakke writes, "The part of the bread-winner . . . is the residual economic role . . . without which self-respect is difficult in a culture which places . . . economic responsibility upon the family."[46] Bernstein also observes how a "father who washed dishes and made beds lost status in the eyes of his wife and children."[47]

Other effects of the Depression were that people stopped educating their children and there were many mothers who found prostitution to be the only way to provide some income for their families.[48] Although the broken family was seen as the immediate cause of social disorder and crime, even when the family was "whole"—that is, when both parents were present—it turned out that they were pursuing money by any means possible. Some families were even urging their young children to steal.[49]

The 1933 Report of the President's Research Committee on Social Trends, published along with the Fifteenth United States Census and various court statistics provides interesting estimates to capture the specificity of the social context.[50] In its findings, not only the broken family, but also the disaffection of children at school, was identified among

30

the causes of criminality (in particular, juvenile criminality). But listlessness was also a direct result of being without food and without shoes and shouldering big problems, outside jobs for those who had any, and street life. It was estimated that forty to seventy percent of juvenile delinquents lived in broken families.[51]

If we read the statistics of the juvenile courts carefully, some interesting differences with regard to male and female behavior and the relative attitude of the judiciary come out. Referring to a sample survey, conducted in 88 courts in 1930, it showed that for boys, apart from generic turbulent behavior, the most common offenses for which they were prosecuted were: theft of various things, burglary, and receiving stolen goods.[52] Car theft, in its own category, also had a high average. For girls, however, the crimes that frequently took them to court were the generic fact of being "ungovernable" and having engaged in sex offenses. Following that, in order of importance, were running away from home and ditching school. Almost nonexistent were burglary, car theft, and armed robbery. Boys and men were not punished for the same "sex offenses" for which juvenile and adult women were arrested and imprisoned.[53] Furthermore, criminology and sociology, similarly investigating the origins of social breakdown in those years, strongly agreed that the broken family would produce the most damage if there was an "immoral mother" in it.[54]

Further clarification should be made about the effects of the crisis on the Black family.

When the crisis arrived, Black people, as we said earlier, constituted only a relatively low percentage of those employed in industry and, despite having inherited the most difficult jobs vis-à-vis whites, they maintained a position of resistance during the 1920s. By the end of these years, those who were not employed in agriculture in the South lived in the slums of cities where reproduction didn't pass through a family structure dependent on a high male wage. Rather, everyone had to support him or herself alone, almost always through "illegal" activities. Oftentimes, it was more likely that the woman helped support the man rather than vice versa.

The peculiar history of Black women, not dependent on a male wage at a mass level, would reveal its impressive potential particularly in the 1960s. It was more likely for Black women, rather than men, to get a paid job. In fact, jobs as waitresses, maids, laundresses, and as workers in sweatshops were destined at a mass level for Black women as well as immigrant women.

Let us now consider some information from Frazier concerning Black communities in the slums:

> ... Some of the men and women of the foregoing type are strangers to the background of the simple-minded peasant Negro from the South. But, it often happens that they are the children of migrants and, having been bred in the slum areas of northern cities, are more sophisticated than migrants from the South. The vast majority of the roving men from the South never get the "break" that would enable them to derive large incomes from preying on men and women. Many of them are reduced to the position of the itinerant bootblacks who may be seen soliciting shines at half-price on the curbs in Negro communities. Usually they manage to find a rooming-house in the Negro slum area and are able to save enough to pay a woman to stay with them for a night. Or they may find some impoverished and lonely woman with whom they live with until one or the other drifts away or the association is ended in violence.[55]

From these references one gets a glimpse of the peculiar social context of the Black community in the slums. It was a context without a family structure supported by the man's income, and where men and women got together for an extremely precarious cohabitation, each party contributing what he or she could in order to survive. However, it was a structure in which poverty, for women, did not translate *tout court* into heavy reliance on men, an unlimited extension of free domestic labor, and sexual discipline.

Even if its characteristics were very different from those of the white family, the Black community in the urban ghettos in the 1920s expressed a peculiar cooperation with regard to its own physical and political reproduction. As Rawick writes:

> The kinship structure that had emerged under slavery, where generalized extended family units allowed for children to be taken care of despite the absence of the biological parents, continued to be operative. Black ghetto children may not always live with their biological parents, but there is almost always some other adult, grandmother, aunt, uncle, or neighbor, willing to step in and raise the child.[56]

As an extension of this cooperation, during those same years, Marcus Garvey's Universal Negro Improvement Association (UNIA) recruited millions of urbanized Black people. The Freedom Halls, managed by the UNIA, provided the Black community with a place to live for nominal rent until they found somewhere more stable to settle, as well as resources and information for finding employment. Above all, the UNIA provided a place of identity and political cohesion. The nationalist proposal, which substantially contained a proposal for autonomy, was able to coalesce the first Black mass movement.

When the crisis exploded in 1929, there was clearly greater uncertainty about the possibility of employed Black people maintaining their jobs. The Unemployment Census of 1931 revealed that among Black workers in the cities, unemployment was twice that among whites. In Detroit, 60 percent of Black workers were unemployed compared to 32 percent of whites. Similarly, in Houston, 35 percent of Black workers were unemployed compared to 18 percent of whites. About half of Black workers in skilled labor lost their jobs.[57] So percentage-wise, Black people were more deeply affected by the crisis than whites, and as we said, were even more discriminated against in welfare plans. It was the impact of the crisis in the South which led to an influx of thousands of Black women and men to northern cities. The most targeted city was Chicago. Here, says Frazier, the Black family structure—as in New York and in general, as in other cities with inflow—was extremely disintegrated.[58] Not only did men and women often migrate alone, i.e., move from South to North outside of family relationships, but it was also unlikely that, having arrived at their destination, they would be able to rebuild family structures or build them anew.

A sample of 115 homeless Black men taken from a survey of 20,000 homeless men in Chicago—of whom 10 percent were Black—revealed that 52 percent had been married, and of these, 75 percent had abandoned their wives. Another survey of 7,560 unmarried Black people who arrived in New York City showed that about 42 percent of them were under 35 years of age. By the time men and women arrived in the northern city they had changed a lot of their southern ways of life, maintains Frazier. Often the men had learned to circumvent the necessity of work by living by their wits. That included gambling, trafficking in stolen goods, engaging in the "numbers" racket, and other types of rackets. Frazier adds: "What is important in regard to these "tribeless" men and women is that they have become purely individuated and have developed a purely "rational" attitude not only toward the physical environment but also toward men and women."[59]

The National Health Survey of 1935–36, conducted by the United States Public Health Service, provides significant data on the living conditions of Black people during the Depression, in particular on housing conditions and health. According to the survey, in cities with fewer than 10,000 inhabitants, 73 percent of whites and 9 percent of Black people had bathrooms in the home. In the period between 1936–40, a report conducted by the Federal Housing Administration shows that 73 percent of homes occupied by Black people in 18 cities had bathrooms that were out of use. In four Southern towns, 60 percent of unaided Black people had no water in their homes for cooking, and 75 percent didn't even have bathrooms, while only 10 percent of white families were deprived of one or the other. The houses were dilapidated. There was more overcrowding than in the homes of whites.

Urbanization brought about a further decline in the Black birth rate, although in some rural areas the rates continued to be relatively high. For example, in Chicago the lowest birth rate was in the "Bright Lights District," where there was a particularly disintegrated social structure.[60] In the center of Harlem, there were only 66.1 births per thousand married women. Regarding these statistics, Frazier writes:

> The disorganized elements in the Negro community are employed sporadically at low wages as unskilled workers or secure a living in criminal activities. They are generally concentrated in areas where there is much overcrowding and an absence of adequate sanitation. Consequently, it is in the most disorganized areas of Negro communities in the cities that one finds the lowest fertility among Negro women.[61]

Abortions were also most frequent in these urban areas. In 1929, there was a rise in illegitimate births of 31.9 per thousand compared to the previous two years. But for Black people, this rise was four and a half times that of whites.[62] Infant mortality, along with childbirth mortality for women, was much more pronounced amongst Black women than whites.[63] The death rate of Black people in 1935 was approximately equal to that of whites in 1916,[64] and the overall conditions of life meant that the highest mortality was among those with chronic diseases—in particular, communicable diseases such as tuberculosis, influenza, pneumonia, and syphilis. This picture of the Black communities, especially within larger cities like Chicago and New York, allows us to see clearly the decimated power of a proletariat that the crisis would push, more and more, towards the North.

THREE

FORMS OF STRUGGLE AND AGGREGATION OF THE UNEMPLOYED

IN THE EARLY DAYS OF THE DEPRESSION, the millions of unemployed thrown on the streets with their families didn't immediately knock at the doors of assistance. That would only have aroused horror, and the desire to stay far away from a system of aid, which was to be provided only for local constituencies, or sometimes at state levels, and inspired by the criteria of "charity."[1] Their real function was to convince people to accept any job, whatever the conditions of work, just to avoid becoming one of those seeking assistance. However, when it came to widowed mothers, the states had been able to negotiate the minefield of money disbursal. In a period which emphasized the social function of the mother—in other words the nature of the work of motherhood—mother and child could be held up as the "deserving core." This kind of support was by no means permissable for the adult male, who, if not working, even if for reasons sometimes recognized as "social," could not appear "deserving" in any way.

Furthermore, before 1929, some cities like New York and Philadelphia were entirely without outdoor relief—that is, relief given to those not residing in a workhouse or institution—owing to legislative statutes that had abolished such assistance since the nineteenth century. Consequently, many preferred to resort to extended branches of the family to look for loans, any kind of help, or in the end, as we have seen, to leave young children with relatives in the rare cases where this was possible. Thousands of young couples returned to live with their parents, who were often unemployed themselves. It was common to see people sleeping wherever there was an empty corner, in the living room, in the kitchen, on the floor.

At first, men were greatly ashamed of being unemployed. They seemed to be revisiting the situation of the crisis of 1873 that their grandparents had already lived through. Some husbands (of course in the early days of the Depression) complained that their wives did not believe that they could not find work, and asked social workers to send someone to explain it to them.[2]

For some time, people were resistant not only to seeking help from local assistance services, but also to the notion of taking different paths from that of honest work, of which there wasn't any. The last act, before resorting to stealing, was a letter to the authorities, usually the governor of the state. It was an act of trust on the part of certain citizens toward the state as a testimony to the social solidity and soundness of values that work and family had previously generated.[3] One of these letters reads:

> This is the first time in my life that I have asked for help, but the way things are now I must. I have been out of work for a long time and my wife is sick in bed and needs medicine, and no money to buy nothing to eat and what is a fellow going to do. I don't want to steal but I won't let my wife and boy cry for something to eat. . . . I am sorry I have to ask you but hunger drives me to do this. I will ask before I steal, as Governor of our State, I beg for help. I am drove to this being out of work, and no money. What is wrong with this country, anyway?[4]

This letter, sent to Governor Pinchot of Pennsylvania, is typical of the correspondence that public authorities received. Besides mentioning the conditions that justified their request for aid, one registers an attitude of people's trust in big government. People did not fundamentally understand what had happened to bring such a disastrous

38

crash so suddenly and violently upon them, and also on the state, from which they began to demand both aid and an explanation. And they also often believed that, through bad choices, they had personally contributed to the terrible fate which was now before them.

In an interview in which he related his personal story, Mr. Grossup, a skilled cabinet maker, told how immediately after being fired after twenty-six years at the Tonti Custom Furniture Company, in a midwestern city of 300,000 inhabitants, he thought that if he had gone to work in the electrical industry, a sector that promised to develop in the future, things would have gone differently.

> It hadn't been so bad at first. Sometimes he would leave the house, all dressed up in his best, and then he'd walk fast with his back very straight, his face carefully held to bright alertness, trying to look as if he were hurrying to a business appointment. But he always ended up in the park. "Something would turn up," he had told his wife, "the President himself says so."[5]

Like him, many others continued to interpret the crisis as a natural disaster that would soon be resolved. Except that instead of ending, it would go from bad to worse every year until 1933.

Grossup's story, only partially recounted here, is a good portrayal of the dynamics of political transformation among the social layers that the crisis doomed to destruction. The Black proletariat, although not yet having the mass power and driving force that it would acheive in the early 1960s, emerged in this period as a living force against the petty-bourgeois, which, closed within itself and facing the same fate of ruthless struggle for survival, headed toward a most profound transformation.

The other significant subject of the story is the wife who, despite her lesser power, hadn't lost so much due to the crisis as to be ashamed of seeking help from neighbors, to keep from being evicted. The typical female figure of those years, who had to get things done in the background while keeping up the pride of the once-breadwinner, was forced at the same time to take initiative in order to handle the situation.

Soon, evidence of the mass dimensions of the unemployment crisis would rouse a new power in the unemployed. As early as 1930, marches and demonstrations were commonplace in major cities and government centers. It was the start of the first mass struggle of the unemployed in the United States. What characterized it was the quick development within the struggle itself of a cooperation between several different layers, which involved the entire neighborhood, at least in places where people had managed to not be uprooted. And soon organizational connections would cross the boundaries of the neighborhood, the city, and the state. There were basically three types of struggles that the unemployed, and women in these families, waged: marches, demonstrations, and attacks on shops—and later, on relief agencies. These included struggles to resist evictions, and struggles against the cutting off of water, gas, and electricity.

The first signs of struggle involved men and women looting for food. In the beginning, not even the owners whose shops were attacked dared to call the police. They didn't want to create an uproar and have the example spread. For the same reason, the press was often silent.

Nevertheless, looting for food seems to have been the most widespread sign of struggle during the early years. In early 1932, a journalist recounted that in New York City, groups of thirty or forty men would show up at one of the big chain grocery stores asking for credit. "When the clerk tells them business is for cash only, they bid him stand aside; they don't want to harm him, but they must have things to eat. They load up and depart."[6]

Bernstein, mentioning other examples of looting for food, states that at least until 1932, this phenomenon took on a national dimension.[7] Bernstein also points out that individual and community relief efforts were likely what kept this practice from becoming more widespread. At this point it is rather difficult to measure the true extent of the phenomenon, especially since, as mentioned just above, the newspapers didn't report the news for fear of helping to encourage the practice. Ortoleva tends toward a rather limited interpretation of these actions, basically providing two possible explanations: one, that the workers affected by the Depression considered it unfair to burden retailers belonging to the same community with their needs, as often they too were impoverished by the Depression and because they had been willing to give them credit to overcome the most difficult moments. Second, in the collective mentality there was an insurmountable barrier, not between legal and illegal behavior, but between "acquisition of wealth through work and parasitism."[8]

41

In 1930, demonstrations of the unemployed exploded in several major cities, including New York, Detroit, Cleveland, Philadelphia, Los Angeles, Chicago, Seattle, Boston, and Milwaukee. These were attended by thousands of protestors, including many women who were wives, sisters, or mothers of the unemployed. The presence of Communists at these events, especially in the early years of the Depression, meant the slogans were at least not exclusively aimed at work that didn't exist. Rather there were chants of: "Work or Wages" and "Don't Starve—Fight."[9] Overall, we can say that the Communists' role in these struggles, like that of the Socialists and Musteists (militants of the American Workers Party led by A. J. Muste), was to help create a context for connection and organization on a national level.[10]

According to Bernstein, on February 11, 1930, 3,000 unemployed men stormed City Hall in Cleveland:

> They dispersed only after the police threatened to spray them with water from fire hoses. Four days later the Council of Unemployed in Philadelphia led a demonstration of 250 persons to City Hall demanding an interview with Mayor Mackey. The police drove them

off. A week later 1,200 jobless men and women marched upon the seat of municipal government in Chicago. Mounted police armed with nightsticks dispersed them as thousands watched from the windows of Loop office buildings. Their leader, Steve Nelson, was arrested. On *February 26* a crowd of 3,000 was repulsed with tear gas before the Los Angeles City Hall.[11]

42

March 6, 1930 was declared "International Day of the Unemployed" by the Communists. There were demonstrations across the country, in which 1.25 million people participated. There were more than 100,000 demonstrators in Detroit, 50,000 in Chicago and as many in Pittsburgh. Crowds of unemployed also gathered in Milwaukee, Cleveland, Los Angeles, San Francisco, Denver, Seattle, and Philadelphia.

In New York City, William Z. Foster spoke to a crowd of 35,000 people in Union Square urging them to march on City Hall. He refused to meet with a select committee and the mayor and so the fighting began. The police, as had happened fifty-six years earlier when they bludgeoned the unemployed gathered in Tompkins Square Park, justified their actions by saying that the unemployed were Communists. "These Communist demonstrations in early 1930," observes Bernstein, "failed to produce the revolution in America," but certainly "bleeding heads converted unemployment from a little-noticed to a page-one problem in every important city in the United States."[12] Clashes with the police had become very harsh by then because the mobilization had spread to the whole country.

Over 4,000 people participated in a series of hunger marches on Washington between 1931 and 1932, approximately half of whom were Black, and their initiative and attack capabilities were evident in all demonstrations. Millions of hungry people were behind them.

Meanwhile, in the South, white and Black sharecroppers were uniting in the Sharecroppers Union. The Black leader of this organization, Ralph Gray, was lynched after a motion was passed calling for international solidarity in the struggle to save the Scottsboro Boys, referring to the nine young Black men who were wrongfully accused of rape in Alabama in 1931. Rape was the accusation most easily made against Black men in the South to violently repress them.

In the same year, farmers from Iowa, Illinois, North Dakota, and New York blocked trucks carrying milk and agricultural products, destroying the products and rendering the truck unusable if they didn't desist. On this front the fighting was also extremely strong. Roadblocks were set up and barricades were built on roads leading to major markets. The truckers who did not desist had stones thrown at their windshields, and faced getting beaten, and having their trucks destroyed.

The thousands of veterans who marched on Washington in the Bonus Army March of May 1932 were owed $50 or $100 as an adjustment to military pay according to a law of 1923.[13] In 1932, those dollars represented a few weeks' victory over hunger. The veterans arrived on foot, in old cars, broken-down trucks and freight trains, stopping passenger trains and asking for rides. Some even came from Alaska. Many brought their wives and children with them. Once they became a large crowd, they were diverted to a flat area beyond the Potomac called Anacostia Flats. In June, they numbered 25,000. They organized themselves into a sort of camp in disastrous conditions.

General Douglas MacArthur, Colonel Dwight Eisenhower and Major George O. Patton led the operation in response to the veterans.

> They arrived late in the afternoon, four troops of cavalry clattering by with drawn sabres, followed by six tanks, with machine guns hooded, and a column of infantry, with fixed bayonets, steel helments, gas masks and at their belts, blue tear-gas bombs.[14]

43

Hoover's unfortunate military victory marked the end of any trace of consent to his authority. If there was little doubt that the vast majority of veterans expressed hostility toward Communist ideology and propaganda, it is equally true that along with the sense of legitimate entitlement with which the veterans had pursued their claim, they conferred no semblance of legitimacy to the state's response, which was not just violent but relied upon unleashed military forces.

The other impressive demonstration, which ended even more bloodily, was on March 7, 1932. This event has come to be known as the Ford Hunger March of 1932. About 85,000 people had lost their jobs and wanted to present a program on the basis of which they could be rehired. There were about 3,000 people marching from Detroit to Dearborn and the demonstration had been authorized. However, when the protestors reached the city limits, the police ordered them to turn back. Leaders of the demonstration incited everyone to maintain "proletarian discipline" but the marchers pressed on.

The violent events that followed are well documented. As Schlesinger Jr. writes:

> The police responded with tear-gas bombs, the crowd with rocks and slag and chunks of frozen mud. The Ford fire department poured freezing water on the marchers through firehoses; then the police opened fire, first with guns and revolvers, later with a machine gun. The crowd finally broke ranks under the shower of bullets. A few tried to carry off the injured; the rest fled down the road, leaving four dead and several wounded behind. Out of the windows over Gate Four of the plant, some Russian technicians, learning Ford's production methods, watched the spectacle. . . . The bodies lay in state two days later under a huge red banner bearing a picture of Lenin and the motto: "Ford Gave Bullets for Bread." The band played the Russian funeral march of 1905 and thousands of Detroit workers followed the coffins. . . .[15]

The year 1932 was a turning point in the organizational experience of Black people as well. After two years of unemployment, a former Black worker in Detroit's Chevrolet plant proclaimed himself Elijah Muhammad and founded the Nation of Islam, thereby marking a turning point in the history of Black nationalism. What this now meant was an urban nationalism, within which there was a positive lack of identification with both the ghetto and the plantation.

The 1932 demonstration in Dearborn marked the resumption of struggles within the factory. Those who had been fired laid out their demands entirely to the factory and presented a definite plan of work in order to be immediately rehired. They didn't believe they had been laid off permanently. Therefore, they didn't look to other unemployed people as companions in their struggle so much as they looked to those who were still employed. If Dearborn reopened a cycle of working-class struggles based on demands within the factory, then let us also look more closely at the demands that inspired the hunger marches, the veterans demonstration in Washington, and the major demonstrations of the unemployed throughout the country. In essence, the questions focused immediately on a direct guarantee of income, both in terms of money and basic necessities, to which the state should commit. Jointly they sought work. But the relationship with the old employers had been permanently discontinued by then. So they looked to the state and to local agencies. The municipal buildings were the physical locations where pressure was concentrated and finally burst. Such a massive request for income, put forth to the state, was an absolute novelty in the history of class struggle within the United States. Income from the state in the form of money and basic necessities represented a new and powerful leap in the demands put forth by the struggle.

Of course, to obtain this, it was not enough to march or simply present oneself to local agencies or the state. It is true that Hoover, through the Emergency Relief

Act in 1932, established the Reconstruction Finance Corporation to loan money to individual states. This was the first response from the federal government to the demonstrations of the unemployed. That is, reinforcement and support on the part of the federal government for the localized responsibility of the states, as an alternative to the lousy system of private charity. But all of that remained on a formal level more than anything else because only a fraction of the money, some $30 million of the $300 million allotted to the states, actually reached them.[16] The largest share went to three major banks, while Hoover's guideline to the country, as we have seen, was an invitation to "spread the work." This basically meant cuts in the working hours and the pay of those who still worked to give a bit of work to the unemployed.

It is clear, then, that a direct mass assault on the agencies and social workers themselves tended primarily to break this deadlock of almost total inactivity by the federal government.[17] The march on Chicago of 5,000 unemployed is exemplary. After being housed in city buildings, the jobless asked for three guaranteed meals a day, free medical care, tobacco twice a week, the right for political organizations to hold meetings on the city's premises, and no discrimination against members of the Unemployed Council. They got what they asked for. But in 1932, when the city administration cut fifty percent of relief funding because it was in dire straits, 25,000 people once again marched and in the end, the city obtained a further loan from the Reconstruction Finance Corporation. The assault on agencies, however, often resulted in arrests, woundings and killings,[18] and as long as Hoover held office, the results obtained by the unemployed in Chicago could hardly be considered a significant response to have obtained at a mass level.

The basic fact was rather that protest was, by now, uniting and multiplying the anger of the jobless, and directing it at the state in order to get a guarantee of income. But the state could not resist any further on that ground. This claim for income, submitted by thousands of demonstrators who even left their places of residence to go and organize others and coordinate with others, was the most profound political class recomposition that the state had ever had to face.

Unquestionably, the crisis of 1929 had triggered a wave of general unemployment that remained endemic to the strategy of accumulation—and indeed deepened following the war. But the relationship between the unemployed and the state, and that between workers and the state, were two sides of the same coin. In fact, from that moment onward, the federal government would irreversibly find itself having to respond to this political question and, at the same time, seeking to make its response an opportunity to control employed and unemployed labor alike.

In the years 1933–1935, the struggles and turmoil continued. While, with the Roosevelt administration, the first significant provisions with regard to relief were passed—the first of which was Federal Emergency Relief Act (FERA)—further specific requests for income were still being carried out. These organized campaigns were capable of gathering together masses not only of unemployed but also of the elderly.

After the Black community, the elderly population was perhaps the hardest hit by the crisis.[19] The most formidable movement to aid the elderly was the Old People's Movement or the Townsend Movement, which derived its name from Francis Everett Townsend, the retired physician and old-age activist who formulated the most advanced pension plan that had ever been conceived. This plan guaranteed a $200 per month pension to everyone over sixty. The fund would be created by national taxes on sales. The Townsend Movement had circles (called Townsend Clubs) organized throughout the country and supporters everywhere who enthusiastically put up Townsend's photo in bars and on public walls.

By 1934, the movement had gathered thousands of demonstrators, who had no objection to the two conditions attached to the pension plan: one, that they did not work; the other, that they spend the entire pension within the month. The proposal was also backed by young people who had elderly relatives dependent on them who they weren't able to support. If in 1928, 30 percent of those over sixty-five were dependent on someone, in 1935 the percentage had risen to 50 percent. And this in a moment in which the proportion of the elderly population was doubled compared to that of 1900.[20]

By 1936, there were 7,000 Townsend Clubs, each with an average membership of 300 people. In total there were two million members. Twenty-five million citizens signed petitions in favor of the Townsend Plan. The power of the movement was such that, when the plan was presented to the House of Representatives in 1934, about 200 Representatives absented themselves and those who had the courage to remain voted against it without a roll-call vote.

Another large plan for guaranteed income was carried forward by the former governor of Louisiana, Huey Long, who jokingly called himself "The Kingfish," and who, for a period, was a supporter of Roosevelt. He was also thought to be a good candidate for the 1936 presidential election, as an alternative to Roosevelt. He was an ambiguous figure, branded more than once as a "fascist," and was assassinated in 1935.

The terms of the ideological and political debate in the U.S. during those years certainly struggled to find their European counterparts. And the same ideological battle from right and left about the character of the New Deal is a macroscopic example of what we mean by this.[21] Louisiana was in dire straits when Long became governor in 1928. It was the state with the lowest literacy rates, in which an estimated one-fifth of white men from the farms could not read or write. No state treated children worse;

they were forced to work extraordinarily long hours in the sugar cane fields, or in the strawberry fields, or in the factories and warehouses where shrimp was stored. The roads were in as bad shape as the schools.[22]

Contrary to the interests of local employers, Long built schools and roads. Long's Share Our Wealth program, launched in 1934 while he held the position of state senator, is usually deemed "populist." In practice, it proposed a guaranteed income from the federal government of $5,000 a year per family. It became popular with the rural whites, whose support he had gained for having the courage to move against the interests of local businessmen opposed to any kind of public work for the people. In his formal announcement of the program in 1934, Long declared:

> Two hundred and fifty-four thousand earnest men and women are now dedicated to an unrelenting fight to divide up the wealth of this Land of Plenty so that children will not starve and their parents beg for crusts.[23]

This echoed his oratorical remarks made on April 4, 1932 before the Senate, where he stated that in 1929, the nation's 504 super-millionaires had made more money individually than the 2.3 million farmers who produced corn and cotton had earned collectively.

After Long's assassination, his legacy was taken up by Gerald L.K. Smith, who joined Francis Townsend and the Reverend Coughlin to form the Union Party.[24] This party presented William Lemke as a presidential candidate in 1936. But the alliance barely functioned due to the programmatic and ideological disagreements which pervaded it, and which led to the clear defeat of the party in 1936. However, the formulation of these guaranteed income programs, and the fight to see them implemented, which brought together millions of elderly and unemployed poor people, constituted an extremely significant movement that went beyond the political defeat that it encountered, just for the enormous breadth of aggregated support it produced.

Demonstrations and assaults on agencies continued all the way up to 1935, that is, even after the first wave of reforms had been passed. On March 19, 1935 the first major Black riot in Harlem was recorded, which, according to Hofstadter, marked a change from the previous demonstrations because it didn't start in response to provocations. It was a direct assault on white property, which destroyed mainly food and clothing stores valued at $2 million.[25]

Along with the direct request for income in the struggles of the unemployed came the strenuous defense of the home and the struggles against the cutting off of gas and electricity. Especially at the beginning, the defense of the home was carried out with great strength under the conviction of being within one's rights, rather than turning to assistance. In these struggles, the Black proletariat showed remarkable initiative. In fact, the struggle against evictions began on the Lower East Side and in Harlem, and soon spread to other cities.[26] In 1930–31, groups of people had already devised different tactics to keep the authorities from throwing the furniture into the street. Fundamentally, it was the presence of a mass of people, who were organized through the Unemployed Councils and were present and ready to fight with police officers and the eviction agents, that managed to prevent it. But it was not an easy victory. In New York, the authorities managed to evict 77,000 families. In Chicago, especially in the Black neighborhood where unemployment was massive and police repression even more brutal, it was extremely difficult to resist the evictions. A fight to defend a home would leave people dead and wounded in the streets.[27] In the countryside, the struggle to defend farms put up for auction was no less harsh.

There were Mr. Grossups who were Iowa farmers, crowding around an auctioneer selling a foreclosed homestead, law-abiding, conservative men who now grimly menaced anyone who bid more than a penny for the foreclosed farm. Pushing about a banker or real estate man about to buy the farm, the farmers often suggestively handled a rope as one of their number made the penny purchase and then returned the farm to its foreclosed owner. Despite the aid of neighbors and penny sales, between 1929 and 1933 some 1,000,000 farmers lost their property through foreclosure.[28]

With regard to gas and electricity being turned off, people organized themselves into "gas teams," that returned gas to the homes, and "electricity teams" that hooked the wires back up to the meters after they had been cut by the local company.

Alongside these fundamental forms of struggle, it is worth noting the numerous forms of self-help cooperatives that were devised and organized by the unemployed in order to survive, particularly in the darkest years, i.e., during the Roosevelt administration. By the end of 1932, there were over one hundred self-help and exchange cooperatives in almost thirty states, many with their own systems of payment in goods or currency. Through these organizations, women and unemployed men came together and exchanged their goods and services: wood, fish, apples, and potatoes in whatever small surpluses existed, in payment for repairs or bills of shoemakers, carpenters, tailors, and laborers who could provide other services. Of these examples, the Unemployed Citizens League of Seattle was one of the most significant. It was organized in twenty-two districts in the state of Washington "and included 13,000 families, with almost 40,000 persons dependent on its self-help programs."[29]

It was called "The Republic of the Penniless." While this was the most famous league, other organizations and collective behaviors based on solidarity experienced remarkable growth and articulation. The Western United States was probably the most affected. Overall, this phenomenon involved more unemployed proletarians than the propaganda of the leftist parties, which often did not even tolerate a solidarity initiative by the Unemployed Councils to raise funds for a neighbor in difficulty. Particular attention has been paid to interpreting these behaviors. For example, it has been pointed out how:

> With the collapse of the credibility of the political system (at both local and federal levels), rather than an alternative political plan (that of the Communists, who became increasingly isolated), a set of pre-political behaviors, so to speak, was established as a counter action, with the community as the center of social relations based on solidarity. At that stage, the unemployed and the proletarians affected by the crisis tended to institute relatively autonomous social structures, avoiding a clash with political power that they sensed they could not win, avoiding being drawn in to opposing the crisis economy with an "economic plan" that was equally abstract and alien, and limiting themselves to the concrete relations of mutual help. . . . It was the rediscovery not so much of the clash between the classes, so much as their differences, their separateness . . . the rediscovery of the proletarian community as the only organized, and possibly economic, horizon (what E. P. Thompson calls "moral economy"), as opposed to a "political economy" and a general organization of life that had gone bankrupt.[30]

The phenomena were defined as "social radicalism" as opposed to "political radicalism," as they were not the result of linear processes of "radicalization" but rather due to fundamental shifts in the collective mentality.[31]

It should be noted that the "do it yourself" attitude exemplified by these cooperatives also included, as the literature of the time lamented, an illegal sector for the extraction and smuggling of coal in Pennsylvania. Brecher writes, "Small teams of unemployed coal miners simply dug small mines on company property and mined out the coal, while others took it by truck to nearby cities and sold it below the commercial rate."[32] In 1934, the extent of this illegal industry could be measured at the production of five million tons of coal worth 45 million dollars, employing twenty thousand men and four thousand vehicles. It should also be noted that, at one point in the illegal extraction, the miners came to use the company's equipment for their own production.[33] However, as Brecher notes, "Local officials would not prosecute the miners, juries would not convict, and jailers would not imprison. When company police tried to stop the bootlegging, the miners defended themselves by force."[34] At one point in the illegal extraction, the miners came to use the company's equipment for their own production.[35] Bernstein addresses the phenomenon of the expansion of illegal practices, saying that questionable methods to get ahead developed rapidly.[36]

53

Regarding the role played by women in the struggles for assistance, and thus for money, in defense of the home, for food, gas, energy, and everything else, some things should be clarified. As we have maintained in the preceding pages, the disruption of the family in the 1930s was a fact suffered by the class, and consequently, the very behavior of family abandonment by the woman, or man, or youth, should be taken in this sense. Forced abandonment heavily necessitated prostitution by mothers, and increased illegitimate births were probably the result of having little chance of a "normal" life. In the same way, the decline in marriages was largely determined by unfavorable conditions. In the struggles for relief in those years there was no possibility for women on a mass level to build an alternative family structure, as would emerge from the movements of the 1960s and '70s. Whether on the issue of relief in the early years of the Depression, or later, the relationship with the struggle in the factory, women moved substantially in defense of the family.[37]

FOUR

FROM HOOVER TO ROOSEVELT

THE HOOVER ADMINISTRATION

This chapter will examine how the state articulated its answer to the crisis and the struggles that followed, giving preference to the area of socioeconomic relief and, more broadly, the reproduction of labor power. It is only relatively recently in Italy that an interest in the reproduction of labor power has developed, while the aspect of the relationship between the state and the employed section of the working class, and thus the very history of collective bargaining, has already attracted considerable attention for years.

This crisis represents the first time that the U.S. federal government was obligated to assume responsibility for the economic well-being of the general population. The assumption of this new responsibility was, as we shall see, very intensive. It was necessary to get from Hoover to Roosevelt, even before the New Deal, for this transformation to begin.

Under Hoover, the state still viewed the masses of the struggling unemployed bearing down on it not as the sign of a new class composition, for whose reproduction the state and capital must necessarily take responsibility, but as the re-emergence of old reserve armies that could be kept at bay with weapons; or, as parasites to which a disinterested stance could be taken. The state hadn't yet seen the necessity of taking direct responsibility for the entire production process, and thus, for the entire process of social reproduction. When the need for this step became clear, the need for the state to revolutionize its entire institutional framework and the functions that each of its organs carries out would be immediately clarified.

The "positive government" that had characterized the state in the previous period—not forgetting the short but exceptional experience of the War Industries Board, extremely significant as a political laboratory—did not carry out the integration of the manufacturing world and the social world. The state, at that time, was able to program social efforts, but it was not able to formulate a comprehensive model of social reproduction; it still placed itself outside of the world of production and reproduction. Consequently, the only sector in which legislative activity of some importance was developed was that of mothers' pensions, and that was relegated to a residual level.

Hoover was the exemplar of the philosophy that had dominated the previous era. He had always described his principles as "true liberalism" against the false liberalism of his critics on the left. It was actually from the previous century's principles of liberalism that he drew inspiration, and that he thought most correct. Precisely for this reason, when the outbreak of the crisis and the problems that emerged from it underscored the necessity of revolutionizing that philosophy, and abandoning the old myths of individualism and complete liberalism, he headed toward political defeat. His downfall coincided with the failure of the world from which he had come. As Hofstadter writes:

> The things Hoover believed in—efficiency, enterprise, opportunity, individualism, substantial *laissez-faire*, personal success, material welfare—were all in the dominant American tradition. The ideas he represented—ideas that to so many people made him seem hateful or ridiculous after 1929—were precisely the same ideas that in the remoter past of the nineteenth century and the more immediate past of the New Era had had an almost irresistible lure for the majority of Americans. In the language of Jefferson, Jackson, and Lincoln these ideas had been fresh and invigorating; in the language of Herbert Hoover they seemed stale and oppressive.[1]

This observation is not surprising if we think of some of the oddly optimistic statements that he frequently made, such as in 1931 shortly after the collapse of the markets: "The fundamental business of the country, that is, the production and distribution of commodities, is on a sound and prosperous basis."[2] Hoover never stopped believing that the crisis had been generated by something outside the very mechanisms of the U.S. economy; he was confident that there were international causes.

Even at the end of October 1930, when the only doors at which the unemployed could knock were those of local or private relief—itself designed essentially to force people into work on whatever terms necessary—Hoover replied to those who had demanded a special session of Congress, reaffirming "his confidence that the nation's 'sense of voluntary organization and community service' could take care of the unemployed."[3] To the President's Emergency Committee for Employment (PECE), which he had reluctantly appointed shortly before, Hoover presented the problem of unemployment as a "local responsibility," while at the same time opposing any concrete proposal for employment.[4] It is evident that, in state matters that followed these events, the part of the political establishment that was most "open" to social problems at that time could only run up against closed doors, since the solution in reality required a radical transformation of the state itself. The problem of unemployment, due to the absolute novelty it represented, was a problem whose solution could not be compatible with any old form of state. Again, it was a problem for which the state had to immediately guarantee social reproduction on a grand scale, regardless of the availability of employment and, in the near future, through the government's capacity to rebuild this employment and these wages in general.

It was a problem for which the prevailing social order, insofar as it took place through the stability of the family, and the family through men's wages, had to rebuild the fundamental pillars on which that model of family stood:

external work, or in any case, an immediate income for the man; and through this, domestic work for the woman.

Hoover's state did not take on any of that. The president chose instead to focus on the problem of drought, which in the summer of 1930 destroyed crops and livestock across the Southwest. In fact, he immediately arranged for a relief program for this problem, asking Congress to allocate funds for government loans to enable farmers to buy seeds, fertilizer, and livestock feed. But when the Democratic senators asked him to allocate funds for the unemployed as well, or to distribute to the unemployed the grain for the livestock, Hoover replied that he found this objectionable.[5] Instead, the decision to "spread the work" appeared to him so commendable that he encouraged people who were struggling with their wages to give a day of their week to the relief committees. Meanwhile, people wrapped themselves in newspapers to keep out the cold, and children couldn't go to school because they were without shoes and coats. As people died of starvation without a roof over their heads, some began inventing jobs that did not otherwise exist. Apple sellers, for instance, were competing to polish apples red. In 1931, Hoover announced that a national study on unemployment had convinced him that local and state organizations needed to be mobilized meet the country's needs, and he appointed a new committee, the President's Organization for Unemployment Relief. Its function was mainly to encourage private charity.

The leaders of the AFL supported Hoover's policy, affirming that prosperity was "just around the corner," and there were no strikes called by the AFL to oppose pay cuts. The AFL had already spoken out violently in 1930 against any form of unemployment insurance, in agreement with the Fordist thesis that state-mandated relief or insurance would transform an aided unemployed person into a "disabled" person dependent on the state. At the 1931 AFL convention, organization president William Green went wild in front of the convention as he warned of catastrophic revolutions coming down on the heads of corporate entrepreneurs if they were not readily co-ordinated.[6] But the AFL merely avoided giving its support to compulsory insurance against unemployment, which was supported instead by Dan Tobin of the machinists union and other, bolder trade unionists. Indeed, the pressure caused by social disorder, and the continuing demonstrations and struggles of the unemployed, by then organized throughout the country, had strongly induced in politics, industry, and agriculture the feeling that revolution might actually explode at any moment. "Many of those who are most boisterous now in clamor for work," said the president of the NAM (National Association of Manufacturers), "have either struck on the jobs they had or don't want to work at all, and are utilizing the occasion to swell the communistic chorus."[7]

59

In 1932, Edward F. McGrady, a conservative representative of the AFL, testified before a Senate committee that despite the sermons of the AFL leaders to urge patience, if something wasn't done and people continued to die of hunger, the doors of revolt would be thrown open. As the struggles of the unemployed—or "crime" as administrative agents often preferred to call it—clearly demonstrated the unsustainability of the situation, even the very cornerstone of the political debate, that is, the necessity of balancing the budget, began to be questioned and attacked. Significantly, McGrady also claimed that "there are another two B's besides Balancing the Budget, and that is to provide Bread and Butter."[8]

Nevertheless, big business still refrained from seeking direct state intervention in the economy. Big business and big industry remained essentially in agreement that there had been many depressions in the last 120 years, that the best way to get rid of business cycles was to show that they were inevitable, and that the government should limit itself to governing and stay out of the economy. The least agreeable point for all of them was precisely benefits for unemployed persons. Henry Ford argued that unemployment insurance would only serve to guarantee that there would always be unemployment. There were others who proposed to feed the unemployed with the waste of restaurants, provided, of course, that they worked for free cutting wood donated by farmers! Henry Ford (who by then had acknowledged giving Hitler financial aid) and the President of the Chamber of Commerce of the United States were in agreement with these assumptions.[9] And the most feared and painful point for all of them was precisely benefits for unemployed persons.

The first significant breakthrough in the industrial and financial world was established instead when the idea of a need for planning began to spread. The shrewdest advocates of the capitalist and political classes began to understand this. "The tragic lack of planning that characterizes the capitalistic system," wrote Paul Mazur of Lehman Brothers in 1931, "is a reflection upon the intelligence of everyone participating in the system."[10] And Bernard Baruch, recalling the example of the War Industries Board, hastened to ask for the suspension of antitrust laws in order to allow "industrial self-government under governmental sanction."[11] It was another overly generic affirmation, considering the necessity by now for the establishment of state responsibility to relaunch and control production. True, they were now addressing the issue, but there lacked the insight that, for the resumption of overall functioning state, "sanctions" would not be enough. The state itself would have to position itself in such a way as to propel and define the terms of development.

The first projects of production planning were delineated by a number of categories that were supposed to coordinate production and consumption and stabilize prices. The very structure of the economy, however—and not only the shape of the state—was an obstacle to the implementation of these plans. After all, the point was not only the more or less extensive coordination of production and control of consumption within the given framework; actually, the relationship between production and the state needed to be revolutionized—and with it, necessarily, the relationship between the reproduction of labor power and the state.

Hoover signed the Emergency Relief Act into law in 1932 without difficulty. While it ostensibly allocated funds for unemployment, in reality the law further deepened the state's attempt to stabilize the economy through the subsidization of large banks. Even at a formal level, it contained not a single contradiction to shake the institutional order. The problem of unemployment still remained primarily a local responsibility, or at most an issue for individual states. The Act only opened up the possibility, more nominal than anything else, for states to push for integration through the Reconstruction Finance Corporation (RFC), in the form of loans from the federal government.

> When Governor Pinchot of Pennsylvania, pointing out that the expenditure of $60 million among the more than one million jobless in his state would give each of them only 13 cents worth of food per day for a year, applied for the sum of $45 million, the RFC, after due deliberation, made about $11 million available. By the end of the year, only $30 million of the $300 million was allotted for relief, and even less for public works.[12]

Even Ogden Mills of the RFC considered it basically a psychological measure. He stated, "its very existence will have a great effect psychologically, and the sooner it is created, the less use we will have to make of it."[13]

Again, in 1932, as the crisis deepened, the unemployed and veterans were in the squares and even the workers began to march threateningly (e.g., the Ford Hunger March at Dearborn in March), but the state didn't change course. Rather, it faced the situation with the Army and the National Guard.

THE NEW DEAL: THE FIRST WELFARE MEASURES

Roosevelt's New Deal represents a move toward a

new form of state based on putting Keynes's proposal into operation, even if only through the massive military investment entailed by World War II. With the destruction-reconstruction cycle of the postwar years, this proposal would actually take off. During this period the master plan to make the relationship between the working class and the capitalist state operate dynamically would begin to take form. Nevertheless, in an unprecedented objective political recomposition during a state of general unemployment, unemployed sections of the working class, alongside those with wages guaranteed through work, immediately turned to the state to take direct responsibility for their reproduction through a mass claim for income.[14] Thus, regarding the unemployed, the state was obligated to anticipate the assumption of direct responsibility for the regulation of class struggle, which only later would articulate the full complexity of its instrumentation, starting with the industrial union. As we have seen, the AFL in 1932 ignored the problem of the unemployed, save for its eschatological predictions about the imminence of revolution, but even the CIO would remain largely unconcerned. It was with the state alone that the new dispute was opened. It was from here, from the area of unemployment, that the state would have to take its first steps in becoming the primary subject charged with the process of reproduction of labor power.

Roosevelt took office in 1933, at a time when states were faced with about fifteen million unemployed and struggled with the depletion of their funds by public aid expenditures, and with the inability to get loans of any substance through the RFC.[15] The average subsidy granted for public aid was about fifty cents per day, per family. In some states, forty percent of residents received aid, and in some counties this figure rose to eighty or even ninety percent of residents. Funds were lacking everywhere, while the protests of the unemployed were rampant and growing.

The first order of political responses is commonly

referred to as the recovery period, in that it was inspired by the urgent need to get out of the crisis in any way and as quickly as possible. Many of these responses would later be cancelled or overturned with the advent of the reform period, or the second New Deal. There would be political continuity—beyond the formal validity of the legislative act containing it—between what was the heart of the early New Deal, namely the famous Section 7a of the National Industrial Recovery Act (NIRA), and the second New Deal, in the sense that the state by then had accepted the redefining of the relationship between capital and labor.[16] The need for collective bargaining, once formally established, would only require the force of the wave of struggles from 1933 to 1937 to convince even the most recalcitrant capital.

63

Likewise, since the state was by then obligated to provide income to the unemployed, there would be great continuity between the Federal Emergency Relief Administration (FERA) and the Social Security Act. Between the revision of the former, in regard to its aspect of provision of direct grants, and the enactment of the latter, after a number of work-aid projects also supported by funds from the FERA, there was the further and more diversified articulation of a protest movement (including the Old People's Movement and Share Our Wealth, as mentioned previously) which showed that, having attained an initial level of income, the unemployed, young and old, were once again struggling to get more.

Congress passed the FERA on May 12, 1933, formally establishing for the first time the government's direct responsibility for the unemployed.[17] An institution of national aid was founded and was allocated $500 million for this purpose.[18] The FERA represented a turning point in the state's response to the pressure exerted by the struggles and social disruption which were, in turn, brought about by mass unemployment. At the same time, the very incidence and diffusion of these struggles, which by then had been going on for four years, in turn laid the groundwork for a potentially dangerous situation in which the provision of direct grants on a massive scale from a single source exposed the federal government to direct assault by mobilized workers.

> It should be added that the government's agrarian policy that was activated in the same year was designed to increase prices by reducing production, which led to the expulsion of many sharecroppers and tenants from the production process, relegating them to public aid. Other plans such as the Tennessee Valley Authority (TVA) openly discriminated against blacks in their hiring policy. Nevertheless, FERA represented a step forward of substantial importance. First, it sanctioned the federal government's responsibilities in the field of public aid for the first time. Second, it extended the concept of public aid beyond the traditional categories of "orphans of deserving widows" to include "all the unemployed and the needy and people dependent on them."[19]

Because the range of recipients was so large, and there was only one center of disbursement, the state would immediately try to reorganize its capacity. The problem, from the perspective of capital, presented itself as the need to empty the demand for income of any further ability to harness the power of social aggregation. Instead, capital worked to transform it into its own instrument for the social control of the unemployed and the redistribution of the wage bill.[20] Gradually, it had to work toward the reconstruction of employment, even if that meant to "fill old bottles with banknotes, bury them at suitable depths in disused coalmines [and] dig the notes up again."[21] There was also the task of rebuilding the family as the fundamental place of the reproduction of work itself. Already family ties had become too disrupted. Such a lengthy separation of men from their families and work risked their becoming unable to reinstate themselves again.

Along with the problem of relaunching production,

rebuilding the family was very much an issue from the beginning of Roosevelt's administration, which in June of 1933 approved the Home Owners' Loan Act that provided funding for mortgages. It was impossible to think of rebuilding and stabilizing the workforce if families could not get a roof over their heads.

At the same time, the Home Owners' Loan Corporation (HOLC)

> averted the threatened collapse of the real estate market and enabled financial institutions to begin to return to the mortgage-lending business. Its example simplified and liberalized methods of real estate financing everywhere in the nation. Most important of all, by enabling thousands of Americans to save their homes, it strengthened their stake both in the existing order and in the New Deal. Probably no single measure consolidated so much middle-class support for the administration.[22]

While FERA began to function as the direct provider of income, preparations began to be made for the first large work plans, particularly those managed by the Civil Works Administration (CWA), established in November 1933. In the various phases of the state's response to the crisis, new links of mediation were formed between the immediate moment of recovery and that of reform. This was tantamount to redefining the functions of the state itself—from mainly being a manager of public order and conflict mediator, as it was under Hoover, to then becoming the organizer of social labor. While recovery had to be unfolded as immediate mass distribution of income, given the size of unemployment and the extension of the struggles, reform was characterized by distribution of income parsed through work. The CWA was only in existence for four months, though at its height it supported as many as 400,000 projects and employed four million people. Approximately one third of those who received assistance from the CWA worked on secondary roads and highways.[23] However, this administration faced many accusations that its interventions were too expensive (in the end costing almost $1 billion) and that it was structured without appropriate mechanisms to avoid causing damage to private enterprise.[24]

The New Deal response was characterized above all with the relaunching of productivity, alongside the state's strengthened role as direct distributor of income. In this sense, the FERA marked a turning point from which, beyond its subsequent modifications and cancellation, there was no going back. Instead, the Social Security Act, which compared to the FERA would represent the transition to a period of reform, would try to reinstate some precise stratifications among the recipients of this income according to their work. This was especially true for pensions and unemployment benefits. At the same time, it would have to extend its scope to include those who were unable to work, and children in need of assistance. The state, in its assumption of an overall responsibility for the reproduction of labor power, was now irremediably constrained by the contradictions that had arisen with the crisis and the struggles that followed.

Even Francis Perkins, who Roosevelt had appointed as head of the Department of Labor and president of the Cabinet Commission for Economic Security, declared she was convinced that it was more important to beat unemployment than to devise stratagems for social insurance.[25] The design of the CWA program was to give employment to four million jobless by December 15, 1933 and by mid-January this goal was far exceeded.

In 1933, intense factory struggles resumed while at the same time "the AFL seemed little more than an association of funeral directors, a group of mutual aid societies of artisans, led by old men whose only concern was to stay on good terms with the employers."[26] With the factories already in turmoil and a union that had lost all representation, if the FERA clashed directly against the entrepreneurs' refusal to admit the need for unemployment benefits, the CWA was liked even less. This was for three reasons: 1) it cost more than direct aid, 2) its work projects were in competition with private enterprise, and 3) the level of wages was much higher than that of the private sector, especially in the South.[27]

On the other hand, the National Industrial Recovery Act (whose famous Section 7a had sanctioned the right of collective bargaining, however far from becoming a general and effective rule), had also endeavored to fix minimum wages for some categories. And this, at least in its intention, should have ended discrimination on the basis of sex and color.

All of the state work projects activated from 1933 onwards excluded the majority of women and led to heavy discrimination against Black workers.[28] Even the recently established right to unionize didn't benefit Black workers due to the fact that they were kept out of the unions themselves. The establishment of the CIO in 1935 did not automatically mean that doors would open wide for Black workers and for women employed outside the home.[29] Between the rhetoric of the CIO representing everyone working in industry and its actual representation of workers lies a history of power differences, both for Black people and for women in industry. Both groups would only begin to see some changes during the Second World War.

With regard to Black people, J. Jacobson notes the CIO's adherence to racial equality was manifested more at a general policy level than through direct action.[30] L. Valtz Mannucci further explains:

> The CIO declares itself to be against racism and attempts to unionize the Black people *where they are already present*, but does not try to change policies on hiring or qualifications used in individual industries in different geographical areas. The authorities cannot risk losing white members by openly opposing the prejudices that they share with the employers.[31]

The FERA and the CWA were not the only aid programs to be implemented with discrimination towards Black people; there was also the Public Works Administration (PWA), a New Deal agency put together by the NIRA in June 1933. The construction sector absorbed a large part of these programs for the construction of roads, airports, etc. They would bring up the new technology used in their sector as a further excuse to not hire Black people, who they claimed had few or no qualifications.[32]

68

As for relief in rural areas of the South, it clashed with the racism of the white land and home owners, who were able to determine the highest levels of arbitrariness in the distribution of aid. Thus, not only was there a higher proportion of white families receiving aid, the levels of aid for Black families were themselves clearly differentiated. In 1935, in ten Southern states—except Kentucky, where 10.9 percent of Black families were assisted as opposed to 17.2 percent of white families—the rate of Black families assisted was less than 10 percent. In twenty-one of the ninety counties in Georgia, Black families receiving aid were less than a quarter of the white ones.

Black families fared better in the South's urban areas. From 22 to 46 percent of Black families in urban areas of sixteen Southern states and the District of Colombia were assisted, as opposed to only 4 to 18 percent of white families. More than half of the Black families in the border towns and about a third in Southern cities received aid. In these places, the percentage of assisted Black people was often four to seven times more than that of whites but in each case, Black families received smaller allowances than the white ones.

In 1935, an average was calculated in thirteen cities in the South of $24.18 for Black families and $29.05 for white families.[33] In cities of the North, where the difficulty for Black people to find work was even more pronounced, the percentage of assisted families was much greater. It was estimated around 52.2 percent.

With the establishment of the Works Progress Administration (WPA), however, their position would have some improvement. In 1937, Black workers constituted 23.3 percent of the total employed in the work plans of the WPA in eleven Southern states. That percentage would rise over the next four years to 26.1 percent in the South (and to 16 percent in the country as a whole).[34]

As for the Civilian Conservation Corps (CCC), Black people were insignificant.[35] Again, this owed to discriminatory practices by aid agencies of the South. Black families would instead gain something from the Farm Security Administration (FSA), but not in proportion to their size as farmers in the South. While Black people accounted for 37 percent of the farmers, only 23 percent of those who received loans from the FSA were Black. They would also get some benefits from the FSA's loan programs to land tenants, designed to allow tenants and sharecroppers to buy a home. About 2,000 Black families benefited from this. In 1939, FSA aid to Black farmers came in the form of rental cooperatives established in that year.[36] Approximately 1,400 Black families were included in the FSA's thirty-two "homestead projects" that involved thirteen Southern states in 1940.

Before 1935, however, the most important form of subsidy that Black families received, at least in the Northern cities where the level of participation in these programs was higher, was for mothers and children in need. This was the starting point from which, in the 1960s, Black women would move into the Welfare Rights Movement with renewed strength and take the relationship between the state and assisted families to a much higher level.

In the meantime, the composition of assisted people had changed. Among the newcomers, a large proportion was formed by office workers who, after four years of unemployment, had used up their savings and could no longer secure private loans. There was much concern among the relief workers about what could happen with such a widespread level of income distribution. On the one hand, there was the old fear of the Communists: "They are very, very busy getting right down among the farmers and working like beavers."[37] On the other, the assisted were becoming "gimmies": "the more you do for the people, the more they demand."[38] Social workers who, unlike in the sixties, were mostly men and not women,[39] said: "they [the assisted] are beginning to regard CWA as their due ... that the Government actually owes it to them. And they want more."[40] Added to this were the complaints of plantation owners in the South who said that aid provisions made it "impossible to get cheap Negro farm labor."[41] A distressed farmer wrote to the governor of Georgia: "I wouldn't plow nobody's mule from sunrise to sunset for 50 cents per day when I could get $1.30 for pretending to work on a DITCH!"[42]

The CWA stood out for offering regularly paid jobs (for thirty-hour work weeks) as well as for assisting the unemployed who, for whatever reason, had refused aid. The FERA had to limit its aid, offering below average wages. The work projects of the CWA were selected primarily with the intention of accelerating employment. Moreover, whereas the CWA designed and implemented its own programs, the FERA only financed state operations. It also performed a significant part of the CWA's program, including projects set up for unemployed office workers. In 1934, the FERA developed new independent programs like the Federal Surplus Relief Corporation through which agricultural products accumulated in the countryside were distributed in cities. It was immediately met with allegations of unfair competition from the private sector, so its effectiveness was limited to distributing surpluses for a total value of only $265 million.[43] In 1935 it was absorbed into the Agricultural Adjustment Administration (AAA).

Another unpopular function of the FERA was its support of the independent production of the unemployed, which was met with immediate resistance from industry. During the crisis, a spontaneous movement

70

had arisen through which the unemployed exchanged goods and services as a form of economic self-help. At one point these independent producers asked the state governments to provide the equipment necessary for fabricating what was needed to live. The state of Ohio was the first to aid this endeavor by providing half a dozen factories. Other states soon followed the example. Unemployed men and women thus produced their own clothing, stoves, furniture, etc.

71

In 1934, it was estimated that 50,000 families across the nation were part of self-help cooperatives of this type. In the autumn of 1934 these initiatives represented 15 percent of the work granted under the auspices of the Emergency Work Relief Program. Because of the hostility of the industrialists, the FERA was only able to grant a little over $3 million in two years to these self-help cooperatives, and by 1935 it was in decline. However, this type of production received more indirect support from the work programs.

The FERA also carried out specific services in rural areas (e.g., the Rural Rehabilitation Division) to strengthen agricultural structures in places where they were already located. The FERA also played a role in attempting to help realize Roosevelt's dream of farming communities based on a decentralized industry and homesteads with small self-sufficient farms. When the CWA was dissolved in 1934 (in large part to serve the interests of employers), the FERA still carried out some of its functions, but with difficulty.

The full activation of the PWA, which had been established in 1933, would launch relief through plans for larger operations.[44] The slowness that characterized the work of this administration—rebuilding at all costs a large mass of wages—was due to sociopolitical rather than economic reasons. The PWA "built roads and highways, sewage systems and water systems, gas plants and electric power plants; schools and courthouses, hospitals and jails; dams and canals, reclamation and irrigation projects, levees and flood control projects, bridges and viaducts, docks and tunnels."[45] It was said that the PWA brought about "a splendidly improved national estate."[46] The politicians who surrounded Roosevelt, however, were not all equally enthusiastic about a similar level of state investment. Lewis Douglas, Director of the Budget, complained, "I see Government expenditures piled upon expenditures, so that paper inflation is inevitable, with a consequent destruction of the middle class."[47] In 1934, Roosevelt defined his position with the following, "that federal direct relief should come to an end on a specified date; that all direct relief thereafter would be the pauper relief supplied by local government; and that Washington should concentrate on giving every employable worker a job through a massive public works effort."[48]

The Works Progress Administration (WPA) was then set up to provide work on public infrastructure projects (in fields not competing with private enterprise) in exchange for what were called "security wages," which were higher than relief wages but lower than established wages in business and industry. This was in contrast to the criteria used by the CWA, which had taken into consideration "family needs." The WPA was formed with the intention of providing jobs for approximately three million unemployed people, but at the same time it set up mechanisms of wage stratification.

> This "security wage" varied with skill and locality and ranged from $19 to $94 a month. . . . At first, hourly wages were below locally prevailing wages, but in 1935, after vigorous protests from organized labor, hours of work were reduced to bring the hourly wage up to the prevailing rate.[49]

In reality, the actual employment that the WPA was able to offer was 2.5 million jobs. The remaining jobseekers were sent back to local and state administrations.

THE NEW DEAL:
TOWARD A SYSTEM OF "SOCIAL SECURITY"

To better appreciate the overall path of struggles and changes in the institutional framework along which social aid and security would develop during the second New Deal, let's refer to some highlights of the workers' struggle.[50] The years after Dearborn in 1932, especially 1933 and 1934, were characterized by a strong resumption of workers' struggles. Workers took full advantage of Section 7a of NIRA despite strong resistance from individual capitalists and the state apparatus. This resistance represented the difficulty of collective capital to affirm its point of view.

NIRA was passed in June 1933. Along with the right of workers to "organize and bargain collectively through representatives of their own choosing and [to] be free from the interference, restraint, or coercion of employers of labor," it established the principle of minimum wage and maximum work hours.[51] Soon after it was passed, struggles in the factories unfolded with particular vehemence.

> In the second half of this year the number of strikes was equal to those of the entire previous year, and the number of workers struggling was three and a half times that of 1932. In 1934, there were 1,856 strikes involving 1,500,000 workers, more than seven percent of employed people. Thus, the number of conflicts was not particularly high but they involved large industries and large categories, steel and automobile workers, Pacific coast dockers, northwestern timber workers and, right up front, the loudest of all, almost 500,000 textile workers with these requests: a thirty-hour work week, a minimum wage of $13, abolition of the stretch-out (the speed-up of the textile industry), and recognition of the United Textile Workers.[52]

Owing to the these struggles, on July 5, 1935, Senator Robert Wagner promulgated a bill, the National Labor

73

Relations Act, better known as the Wagner Act, which reconfirmed the right of workers to bargain collectively and to strike. Moreover, it provided mechanisms for sanctions against employers who did not respect this right. The National Labor Relations Board was established for this purpose and, through its direct actions or through the regular courts, it had the power to compel employers to respect the law. It would take another two years of struggle, and a wave of factory occupations in 1937, before the Supreme Court dropped its accusations that the Wagner Act was unconstitutional, encouraging employers to change their attitude.[53]

1935 is commonly referred to as the year the New Deal "took off." It was certainly the year in which the relationship between state and working class became more direct. The CIO was founded that year, and at its convention in Atlantic City, John Lewis famously punched the carpenters' representative, William Hutcheson. This gesture, which seemed more premeditated than spontaneous, marked the break between the old AFL craft union and the new CIO industrial union. At first, the CIO was only meant to be a branch within the AFL to promote organization in mass sectors. In 1936, the Executive Council suspended the ten federations who were affiliated with the CIO, comprising a total of 10 million members. In 1937, the year of the occupations in factories and elsewhere, the number of CIO affiliates exceeded that of the AFL.[54] In 1938, the Committee became the Congress for Industrial Organization. The relationship between state and class became more direct, and the struggles of the unemployed brought this relationship closer than it had ever been before. A first level of responsibility of the U.S. state for the reproduction of labor power was founded primarily through the direct provision of income. At this point there was no going back from this allocation of responsibility.

It was precisely the intersection of the struggle of the unemployed and the struggle in the factory, which exploded violently after the first years of the crisis, that forced the state to reformulate its answer to questions of labor management. The struggle of the unemployed had given a hint to those who had managed to keep their jobs. The workers' battle for the regulation of layoffs, so that they would be based on clear and objective criteria, and above all the observance of the rule of seniority, were direct results of this hint. At a time when job insecurity was perceived as a daily risk for each worker, it meant putting an end to the will of employers and bosses with regard to layoffs and recalls. And it was with the industrial union in those years that the rule of seniority became a defining feature of American working life.[55] For the worker, it meant no longer having to rely on one's own individual resources against the risk of becoming unemployed, or of aging without any support. *Wages, however high, had proven to be insufficient on their own to ensure some security of life.* The family, with young children who supported the elderly, with a shrewd wife who managed spending and saving, was likely to vanish the moment the young man lost his job. The state was called to take account for this risk. The Social Security Act marked this turning point.

Enacted in 1935, the Act articulates the state's responsibility to workers in the incident of unemployment, old age or the inability to work, and the need to provide for aid to children (usually when there is only one parent). With regard to unemployment, at the urging of the federal government, programs were undertaken by individual states. Within them, employers had to pay the state a share proportional to the wages paid, and another share to the federal government. The latter was intended to form a national fund from which aid would be drawn by the individual states for administrative expenses of the programs themselves. This insurance system, however, mainly covered those workers involved in industry and commerce.[56]

With regard to old age pensions, for the first time the federal government assumed the responsibility of creating a pension system that would be administered by the Federal Social Security Board. Based on contributions from employers and workers, it paid a pension starting at sixty-five years of age. Several categories were still excluded, however: agricultural workers, domestic service workers, seamen, temporary workers, public employees (from the federal level to state to local governments), employees of religious, charitable, scientific, literary, and educational institutions. Pensions with contributions made starting in 1937 would be collectible only in 1942. A separate scheme was planned for the pensions of railroad workers who had already obtained provisions through the Railroad Employees' Retirement Act in 1934.

The elderly and those already poor before 1942, or otherwise deemed not entitled to a pension under the new system, were covered instead by the Old Age Assistance Program. With it, the Federal Treasury subsidized states so that they could carry out measures for older people who did not fit into the pension program administered by the Federal Social Security Board.[57]

In addition to assistance for the unemployed and the elderly, assistance for needy children was instituted through the Aid to Dependent Children (ADC) program, along with assistance for the blind and physically disabled, and for individuals otherwise permanently unable to work. A number of different services related particularly to health were also undertaken.[58]

Compared with mothers' pensions, primarily designed for widows with children, the establishment of the ADC represented a significant enlargement of welfare. The ADC intended to cover needy children in general, almost always in families headed by single parents, and a large proportion of the subsidy was paid directly by the federal government.

The legislation on mothers' pensions, as we have seen, had special importance in the period before the crisis, and above all, bore the criteria for subsequent provisions of assistance. It encountered some limitations with regard to methods used for determining who was entitled to support. For example, there were local administrations that tended to take a merit-based approach to allocations. That is, they evaluated the good conduct of the mother rather than the objective condition of need. By worrying more about "rehabilitating" the family than rescuing it, the scope of entitled claimants was kept small and heavily conditioned.[59]

However, this further step into the system of child care was evidently determined by the pressure exerted on agencies by mothers who, at the mass level, found themselves unable to rely on male wages. This struggle was extremely important because it broke ground upon which a new phase of struggle would be established in the 1960s, when women professed to reject the label of "assistance" for the government money they received, instead claiming it as wages for the work of raising children.[60] In the 1970s, although it was a period of crisis and limited circulation of struggles, the steadfastness of women's responses would further deepen in this area, particularly the refusal to bind maternity to the family regime.[61]

Another noticeable change in the overall framework of responsibility for aid, by local and state agencies as well as the federal government, was its extension to various disabled groups. It thereby delegated to the government, albeit partially, responsibility for the reproduction of labor power not only for those temporarily out of employment, but also for those who could not in any case be employed.

The Social Security Act consolidated, in terms of guaranteed income, the state response to the overall impact of the struggles of the unemployed and the workers, and the women with them. This Act established and coordinated, for the first time, overall mechanisms for guaranteeing reproduction which affected not only the matters of active labor power in periods when it was not directly involved in the production cycle, but also sectors of labor power that would be outside production in any case.

But the full significance of this state response must be contextualized and understood in relation to the fact that shortly thereafter, in 1937, the Supreme Court was finally forced to capitulate on the issue of minimum wage. In 1938, the Fair Labor Standards Act (FLSA) definitively established a hike in the minimum wage from 25 cents to 40 cents an hour, to be completed within seven years.[62] Also, the maximum work week would be reduced from 44 hours in 1939, to 42 hours in 1941, to 40 hours after that for all workers.

Nevertheless, the legislative process that defined the substantive shift forced onto the capitalist state by the working class came to an end with the FLSA. The struggle of the unemployed triggered a new strength in, and above all a new perspective for, the workers' struggle. It would be this constituent power that would definitively make individual capitalists give in and accept the new function and form of the state. In this period, capital and class conflicts objectively expanded the field of struggle and broke ground for new state activity within these conflicts. Specifically, social aid and security was destined to become the primary place of conflict between the two fronts in the following decades. As such, the period in which the family functioned as the site of the overall reproduction of workers also ends here. From the Great Depression onward, the family no longer functioned as the solitary center of a reproductive universe, but rather as a necessary and invariant pole with respect to possibilities for the development of reproductive functions by the state itself.

FIVE

WOMEN BETWEEN FAMILY, WELFARE, AND PAID LABOR

To further detail how, in Roosevelt's project, the state aspired to promote the consolidation of the family, we must extend our focus beyond social assistance and social security to the labor market and the relative composition of male and female employment. We must also look specifically to women's actions in struggle and resistance during the Depression.

The process of consolidating the family institution was more of an intention during the 1930s than an actual fact, as the New Deal wouldn't really take off until the Second World War and the postwar period.[1] However, this process would be interrupted by the need to employ women on a mass level during the war. This interruption would determine an irresolvable contradiction in the female experience between domestic labor and work outside the home—despite the fact that in the 1950s, the state would again propose the further strengthening of the family, primarily through a policy to get women out of the labor market.[2]

WOMEN'S ACTIONS IN RESISTANCE AND STRUGGLE DURING THE DEPRESSION

In the darkest years following the onset of the crisis, women were always "on duty," even if they weren't a leading force on the relief front and acted primarily "in defense of the family," both in those years and those immediately following. It is interesting to note that, perhaps because they had never known the levels of confinement thrust upon their European counterparts in the same period, and subsequently did not identify as substantially with the family, women in the U.S. were often remarkably determined to defend their *own* living conditions, whether inside or outside the family.

There are two principal areas of women's experiences that we have to examine. The first involves women who were not employed outside the home—which, as we know, was the vast majority—and who fought alongside men who were dependent on relief or on an employer. The other involves women employed in jobs outside the home, who, because they had no mass power, paid the price, along with Black communities, for a restratification of class that could no longer base itself on qualification, and would instead be imposed on the basis of color and sex. Let us start with the first group. They were certainly not the "nagging wives and bawling children" depicted by Fine, who the workers occupying the factories would have been glad to be free of.[3] By now it is fairly well known how the wives operated around the occupied factories. Consider the occupation of the General Motors factories in Flint, also known as the Flint Sit-down Strike, 1936–1937. A street dance in front of Fisher Body No. 2 on New Year's Eve 1937 demonstrated that the women and not just the men enjoyed the new sociality that the struggle in the factory had opened. About fifty women came together to form a Women's Auxiliary to support the men inside and outside the factories.[4] The Auxiliary took on the tasks of forming picket lines, organizing day care centers for mothers involved in strike duty, collecting food and money, and contacting the sit-down "widows," i.e., those women who felt greatly weakened by the strike, and encouraging them to mobilize.

Genora Johnson, the twenty-three-year-old wife of one of the leaders of the struggle, decided to form, in addition to the Auxiliary, another body of "courageous women" who would fight with the men if needed. Fifty volunteers came together and the group quickly numbered 350. Thus the Women's Emergency Brigade was formed. It was organized according to semi-military criteria with a commander in chief, Genora, and captains. Genora declared: "We will form a line around the men, and if the police want to fire then they'll just have to fire into us."[5]

Similar organizations were created in Detroit, Cleveland, and Toledo and had a significant effect on the men who fought in the factory. Certainly those strikes and occupations could not have carried on for so long without such women's organizations backing them. These organizations had to radically change the methods of carrying out domestic work and developed a series of strategic moves within the occupation in order to continue the strike.

In Flint, the wives of the workers simulated a demonstration for International Women's Day in order to divert police attention from the occupation of the factory. Fourteen women were injured as they brought lunch into the factory. They broke windows from the outside to prevent tear gas from suffocating those inside. They also organized themselves to provide medical assistance. Obviously they felt themselves changed by such an experience. The wife of a striker said: "I'm living for the first time with a definite goal. . . . Just being a woman isn't enough anymore. I want to be a human being with the right to think for myself."[6] A few weeks after the end of strike, another woman said: "Women who only yesterday were horrified at unionism, who felt inferior to the task of organizing, speaking, leading, have, as if overnight, become the spearhead in the battle of unionism."[7] It's a classic story, but with a force and an articulation that is worth understanding better. What is most interesting is not only the "courageous women" organized in a semi-military way—whose actions constitute a major breaking point in staying at home and being controlled by men—but also the resolve that ran through the women's support of the factory struggle to ensure that the strike would not simply result in a worsening of domestic work.

While, there was a great deal of cooperation around the occupation of General Motors in Flint, what happened in Bloomington, Illinois was quite different. The wives of the strikers went to the occupied factory and refused to prepare meals, wash dishes, or even answer the doorbell until their husbands had given them more money. Despite the paucity of information about the struggles of women in those years, it would be impossible to concede that these were just isolated examples.[8] Moreover, women weren't just out of the house beside the men. They had also decided not to be overwhelmed by the worsening of domestic work at home, and so these women maintained a stiff resolve in response to both the men and the relief agencies.

1937 was the year when not only male workers but also women led sit-downs throughout the country. They sat down in relief offices, factories, offices, cafes and bars, and many other workplaces. It was the year in which the aggressiveness of bargaining for living conditions, and therefore for the conditions of domestic work, lay side by side with the aggressive bargaining for work outside the home. In Detroit, thirty-five women barricaded themselves in a relief office asking that the supervisor be removed, and that a committee meet with the new supervisor to determine the requisites of the families entitled to relief. That same year, thirteen young women occupied another agency in Detroit where they had paid an enrollment fee to get work which they had not obtained. In New York City, relief agencies were occupied by women and men in response to expropriated homes and property, or for fires, for which they always demanded money and goods. In the Bronx twenty-four women held an occupation to prevent twenty-five policemen from evicting their neighbors.[9]

Women students even sat down to protest against school regulations.[10] Sit-downs were used with particular frequency in stores, where it had been easy to replace staff during strikes. Indeed, women sat down in two Woolworth stores in New York City, and the same thing happened in five large F. & W. Grand warehouses.[11] In C.G. Murphy stores in Pittsburgh, because there were no chairs to sit-down on, 150 female shop assistants and twenty-five warehouse boys went on a "folded-arms strike" for more wages and fewer work hours.[12] Occupations and strikes also occurred in the service sector: among the many examples are neighborhood laundries (thirty-five women occupied Durable Laundry) and hospital laundries and kitchens (e.g., in the Hospital for Joint Diseases in New York, and the Brooklyn Jewish Hospital).[13]

Indeed, sit-downs were discovered and used by many sectors of society. They were even performed by those who had jobs in the WPA, prisoners in prisons, and children in movie theaters.[14] It was a form of struggle used not only against the individual owner of a factory (in which the sit-down directly countered "the boredom, degradation and isolation of the factory"), but ultimately, against the weight of work and discipline in general.[15] 1937 was the year that defending quality of life, and bargaining for outside work for women, were particularly linked. But it was itself a particular moment, sustained by the mass strength of the major strikes and the occupations of the industrial giants.[16]

WOMEN AND PAID LABOR

According to the Census of 1930, there were approximately 10.6 million women employed compared with approximately 38 million men. Female workers were generally younger than their male counterparts, and unmarried. 17.1 percent were Black women and 10.8 percent were white female immigrants, whereas, of the men employed, 9.6 percent were Black and 16.4 percent were white male immigrants. From 1930 to 1940, the percentage of female employment relative to the three major sectors of white-collar, personal and domestic service, and manual and semi-skilled labor, varied respectively from 44.0 percent to 44.9 percent, from 29.6 percent to 28.9 percent, and from 26.5 percent to 23.9 percent.[17] The female labor force was concentrated for the most part in the white-collar and personal and domestic service sectors. Many women belonging to this category held jobs such as hairdressers, manicurists, midwives, general nurses, and elevator operators. Included in this sector were women who ran laundries, worked in hospitals or other institutions, and managed hotels and restaurants. Within the industrial field, women were employed mainly in textiles, clothing, leather, tobacco, and food.[18] Because of the different scope of women's employment compared with that of men's, it seems that women were less affected by unemployment during this time. In 1930, for instance, the female unemployment rate was 4.7% as opposed to the male rate of 7.1%.

Neverthless, in the years following 1929, it seems very likely that female unemployment worsened compared with that of male unemployment, and there was also a significant return of Black women to paid domestic labor.[19] If female unemployment in industry represented the continuation of trends already in place, the slowing down of female employment in the white-collar and professional work category was new with respect to the previous period in these areas. Thus it was a more significant indicator of the effects that the Depression had on some aspects of female employment. The personal and domestic service sector saw especially significant changes within it. In 1937 there was thought to be a total of three million unemployed women out of a reputed eleven million women in the available work force. Another 1.5 million women had only part-time or occasional work.[20]

As for wage discrimination between men and women, the disparity was around 30 to 50 percent. Women were destined for the lesser paid jobs in any case as a consequence of the restructuring of the labor market, starting with restrictions on immigration that intensified alongside the standardization of factory work. Wage discrimination was far worse for Black women. In 1935 and 1936, a survey of the Women's Bureau of the Federal Department of Labor on women's wages in Arkansas and Tennessee recorded that, if white women had a salary equal to 64.2 percent that of white men in the former state, and 75.9 percent in the latter, that of Black women was 61.7 percent and 54.2 percent respectively of that of Black men.[21]

To give an idea of women's wages in key industrial sectors in 1937: in textiles, men earned 60.4 cents an hour and women 44.6 cents; in apparel, men earned 93.8 cents and women 54.7 cents; in the food industry, 64.2 cents and 42.2 cents respectively; in leather, 60.6 cents and 42.1 cents respectively; in tobacco, 52.6 cents and 41.6 cents; laundries, 58.8 cents and 34.2 cents; and in dry cleaning, 61.7 cents and 39.9 cents respectively. Women's wages in the service sector in the same year were as follows: in stores, a week's salary was $13.60; in laundries, $9.10; in dry cleaners, $12.65; in hotels, $8.20; in restaurants, $8.65. Just as in industrial sectors, wage discrimination also existed in these types of employment.[22]

The wages of women and children had dropped alarmingly with the Depression.

> Sweatshops were springing up on every side. Child labor was coming back. The Pennsylvania Department of Labor and Industry reported that half the women in the textile and clothing industries were earning less than $6.58 a week, and 20 per cent less than $5. In Fall River, Massachusetts, more than half the employees in a garment factory were getting fifteen cents an hour or less. At the same time, the work week in some states was lengthening to sixty, sixty-five, even seventy hours.[23]

The Consumers' League of Massachusetts uncovered factories in the apparel industry that were paying their workers one cent per hour. Even worse, some workers were paid nothing for a period of apprenticeship, after which they were fired so that others could work for a "trial" period. In Tennessee, women in textile factories were paid $2.39 for a fifty-hour week and in Connecticut, the Commissioner of Labor recorded more than 100 factories that hired girls for between 60 cents and $1.10 for a fifty-five-hour week.[24]

Clearly, only during certain times of resurgence of factory struggles were these women able to fight with some power. And the struggles went on even in areas such as laundries, housekeeping, beauty salons. While the AFL remained uninterested in women, the CIO, which was supposed to be the mass industrial union and a union for women as well, ran up against the fact that there was not a considerable presence of women in leading industries. A certain amount of women's unionization went on in the clothing industry. However, it is certain that neither the AFL nor the CIO bothered to take serious account of their female members.[25]

As the Depression went on, the search for employment by many women was predicated on the fact that their husbands had been laid off and, given occupational segregation, they hoped to find work. However, many declared that women were taking away men's jobs and argued that the massive scale of male unemployment was due to women's entry into the labor market during previous years. In response to such complaints raised throughout the country, the National Industrial Conference Board published a study in 1936 entitled "Women Workers and Labor Supply," which revealed that there was no proof that employed women were taking jobs away from men.[26]

Even so, many states brought back old laws requiring the dismissal of teachers and women employed in the civil service on account of marriage.[27] The AFL leadership opted to support discrimination with regards to hiring women whose husbands already had steady jobs.[28] Despite these measures, the *increase* in the percentage of *employed married women* was one of the most significant facts of the period of the Depression. It went from 11.7 percent in 1930 to 15.3 percent in 1940, a significant leap if we consider the trend of the previous twenty-year period.[29]

Prominent feminist union leader Rose Schneiderman's prediction in the 1920s that these women did not seem destined to stay in the labor market had only temporarily proven true. As a a study conducted in 1939 found, more and more married women were working outside the home, primarily in response to family needs.[30] Nevertheless, the recrimination for their double work was heavy indeed. Francis Perkins, U.S. Secretary of Labor from 1933–1945, "denounced the rich 'pin-money worker' as a 'menace to society, [and] a selfish, short-sighted creature, who ought to be ashamed of herself.'"[31] But it is unclear how rich Francis Perkins's "short-sighted creature" was. If she really was wealthy, it seems unlikely that she would take a job designated for women in situations of real need. Instead it is significant that this theory of the pin-money worker was one of the most serious obstacles that the Women's Bureau claimed to face.[32] Experiments and studies, such as that of Mrs. Borsodi in 1935, whose husband was the leader of the Homestead Movement during the Depression, were devised to prove that women with an outside job would earn more by staying home.[33]

On June 30, 1932, Congress voted for the Federal Economy Act, which prohibited the employment of two members of the same family in government service. In practice, it was directed at married women. And in fact, women represented two thirds of the 1,603 people laid off until 1935 when the act was annulled.[34] Because discriminatory practices against married women were carried out both in public and private sectors, we can assume that if such practices had not been implemented, the percentage of their employment would have been substantially higher.

Despite the campaign to lay the blame on married women working outside the home, this situation actually made the 1930s a very important benchmark in the emergence of a new urban family structure, especially amongst families from waves of immigration of previous decades and from rural areas of the United States who had migrated in the early 1920s. These were families who, to varying degrees, had been emancipated from parental hierarchies and traditional values, who now had to assemble a new type of familial relationship influenced by the largely democratizing force of consumption. The new socioeconomic reality prescribed a partnership that tended towards more parity between husbands and wives.

With rampant unemployment threatening to seriously compromise the hierarchy and entrenched differentiation underlying marital relations, the employment of married women in many cases actually galvanized the family, acting as a cohesive force despite the tensions involved. These tensions were due mainly to men's unemployment, but also to the fact that the domestic workload for women had worsened.[35] The point of maximum family breakdown came when women could not find jobs or when their jobs paid an insufficient wage level.

Some further details should be given with respect to women's work outside the home, relative to the support that women received from the Women's Trade Union League as they had during the 1920s. Such activity, albeit brief, gives some indication of the levels reached by many women's struggles for outside work during those years.

In the period before the Depression, the relationship between the League and the AFL had been more one of support by the League for union initiatives rather than vice versa. If the League called for strikes or mobilization, the union rarely moved to support them. In fact, from 1929 to 1939 the League received no support from unions, not even financial help. Consequently, it found itself somewhat hampered in managing its normal liaison activities across the country and was unable to organize national conferences for the entire decade.[36]

When the Federal Emergency Relief Act was founded, the League asked in vain that work plans be prepared for women who had been laid off as well. But it was very difficult for women to fit into these plans—except for some absorption in the Civil Works Administration and an area reserved for them in the Works Progress Administration—because it was assumed that they had no dependents. The League had to give up its request for jobs and accept the distribution of free food, and at most, the organization of some sewing work.[37]

During the late 1930s, the League continued to fight strenuously on the issues of the minimum wage and working hours. A survey carried out at the League's behest on workers' wages in various industries in Chicago showed that 55 percent of working women earned less than $2.50 a week and young girls often worked for 72 hours per week. In 1933, New York ushered in a new minimum wage law which "declared it 'against public policy' for any employer to pay women and minors a wage less than 'the fair and reasonable value of services rendered' or less than 'sufficient to meet the ultimate cost of living necessary to health.'"[38] The first sectors to benefit from this law were those that the League had always fought to get some regulation for: the laundry industry and hotel and restaurant services. Women working in beauty salons would have been next to receive its benefits, but in 1936 the Supreme Court issued a ruling on the unconstitutionality of defining a minimum wage.[39]

As for the work week, from 1932 to 1934 the League tried very hard to ensure amendments to the fourty-eight-hour law that would have completely eliminated overtime. The need for this became evident after the Court of Appeals of New York had decided in the summer of 1929 that factory owners in the industrial and commercial sectors were not obligated to give employed women their one half-day off per week (as the law intended) if they used the seventy-eight overtime hours allowed by the same law. Having obtained the amendment of this law, the League worked on other projects to achieve regulation of work hours in specific sectors such as hotels, restaurants, and domestic service.[40]

The League also took particular interest in women's working conditions in the home, which had worsened following the cancellation of the National Industrial Recovery Act in 1935.[41] The League supported the Federal Maternity Law until the passage of the Social Security Act, which it deemed to be, in some ways, a better solution to the problem. It supported the need for the unionization of women in the automotive and rubber sectors and the strikes of women textile workers both in 1930 (4,000 workers in Denver), and in 1934 during the general strike, particularly in Alabama.[42] It also worked hard to support the strikes of the women in the clothing sector together with the International Ladies' Garment Workers' Union. The WTUL's work to organize hotel maids in 1939 resulted in the possibility of their having a regular contract in thirty-three hotels in New York. Contracts were also stipulated for beauty salon workers.[43]

These are only a few references to the League's activity, but they show the support the League continued to give to women belonging to the ranks of low-wage employment, who had less protection in regard to working conditions and the hardest material conditions of life. Importantly, the domestic service sector would not be covered by the Fair Labor Standards Act and the possibility of unionization, as represented by the formation of the CIO in 1935, did not include workers in either the domestic or service sector.

TOWARDS STRENGTHENING THE FAMILY

It would appear that the family, or the home, was the only "job" that the New Deal recognized for women in the 1930s. In this regard it's worth specifying some further aspects of its welfare policy.

Some 398,000 women were employed in the Works Progress Administration. A certain proportion were white-collar workers with clerical duties. Most of the others, approximately 170,000, were taken on by the Household Service Demonstration Project as instructors, teaching women how to prepare and serve meals, how to take care of the house, look after children, do the washing, ironing, and grocery shopping. Another 30,000, those who had no particular qualifications, were directly involved in programs to assist families at home, those who needed help due to sickness or other reasons. Not only were women's positions a reflection of their exclusive role as housewives, *none of the courses even provided any specialization that could be used in other fields of work.*[44]

Nevertheless the domestic role of women took on new meanings throughout the 1930s. For instance, the woman's responsibility for the family involved new and more complex tasks. While the number of children continued to decline, in part as a result of the spread of birth control "clinics," the "profession" of parent became more and more problematized. In 1930, training courses for parents were active in twenty-two states.[45] Six universities and two schools provided professional degrees in social work for those who specialized in teaching how to be parents. The proliferation of such initiatives—which included discussion groups, lectures, and newspaper articles—tended increasingly to divert attention from the materiality of domestic work.[46] Instead, women's energies were redirected toward new duties involving the psychological reproduction, disciplining, and socialization of various members of the family.

Likewise in the social sciences, the need was felt to study sexuality with a view to its more adequate development within the new canons of family functioning.[47] In 1938, A.C. Kinsey started his famous survey project on the sexual behavior of American men and women.[48] One important result of this study is that women themselves were increasingly blamed for their sexual nonproductivity.

Moreover, if the proposition of the more complex figure of wife and mother was directed primarily at middle-class women, it nevertheless intended to serve as a model for all women, directed equally to first generation Americans and to women recently arrived from rural

91

areas. Even those who carried out the material tasks of domestic labor in the worst of conditions were not exempt from comparison with their middle-class counterparts.[49]

With regard to the family home, there were still some aspects of the federal government policy that showed its intent to rebuild and stabilize families disrupted by the Depression as soon as possible. Roosevelt's New Deal marked an important turning point. Groups that had done intellectual studies in the field of urban planning in the 1920s, such as the Regional Planning Association of America (RPAA), found outlets for their plans in the New Deal.[50]

92

> Economists were not asking for just a federal policy of intervention, they outlined a turning point: the system should be guided by the question of mass consumption. The theme of mass housing should be shaken up by favoring the development of sub-sidized municipal housing and financial assistance from the federal government for slum clearance and working-class housing.[51]

Roosevelt's administration promoted and financed the construction of single-family homes. From 1935 onward, the United States would definitively be at the forefront of architectural design and planning with respect to the scientific management of the home. While in Europe the focus was more on the home as a whole entity, American design was characterized by a focus on the kitchen. Since it was clear by then that households would rely less on domestic service, for the most part the kitchen was designed for small spaces.[52] The General Electric Co. and Westinghouse Electric Co. founded special schools for the culinary arts and introduced new electric or gas stoves for the home, which women were nevertheless reluctant to buy, primarily because it meant taking on a new appren-ticeship for another line of work.[53] On the other hand, not only was the preparation and cooking of food greatly streamlined because refrigerators were now widely available in American homes, but so too were the tasks of cleaning the house and washing clothes. There was also the first commercial sale of frozen foods that would, not surprisingly, take off with World War II.[54]

As early as the 1920s, technological innovation tended to streamline management of the material duties of domestic labor, shortening the time it took to perform each task. Clearly, this process was put in place to "free" women so that they could dedicate themselves more to the psychological and affective work of reproducing labor power. The social sciences, which in 1937 had the year of their greatest flourishing, agreed and cooperated on this matter.

CONCLUSIONS

With the New Deal, the state's primary goal was to make *wages and their increase* available on a *general* social level. Our analysis began with the Five-Dollar Day, emphasizing the *relative generality* of this agreement despite the strict selection criteria of beneficiaries and the many conditions attached to receiving these benefits, which could be investigated directly by the employers' agents.[55] Now, on the one side, there is the class as a whole that is directly "entitled" to a certain level of wages for which it negotiates collectively through the union. On the other, there is no longer the individual capitalist but the state as the intelligence of collective capital that, through the New Deal, must ensure not only an increase in wages— that is proportionate to the state's investments—but also an adequate mass of wages.

Likewise, Roosevelt's New Deal involved the establishment and articulation of the state's role as guarantor of insurance. The need for this arose from new developments in industry whereby technological innovations and consequent structural reorganization shortened the length of the production cycle compared with the past. One must keep in mind how the proposals that Keynes made in those years were all related to the realization that not only was it necessary to get out of the crisis quickly, but that the length of development trends would henceforth be changed. From these different conditions of capitalist development came the need for the state's presence in social security, no longer as residual intervention but as a function entirely within the plan of the New Deal, and as an extension of this, there was the need to emphasize the role of the family and the woman.

Women were primarily delegated the *responsibility of ensuring the real capacity of wage growth*. Their function as housewives and their domestic work were essential to this. Even faced with the risk of unemployment—endemic to the new modalities of the production cycle—it was up to the woman, as housewife, to ensure a level and continuity of reintegration of labor power for which an unemployment check alone would not be enough. In the overall task of defending the purchasing power of wages, reabsorbing and reproducing individuals not immediately active, successfully producing new labor power and reproducing the active labor power, and therefore defending the capacity of consumption in general, the family functioned at the center of the Roosevelt's New Deal.

Similar considerations applied to other aspects of social security. Work within the family unit consistently ensured the first level of the reintegration of labor power. In comparison, state disbursements could only play a complementary role. At this point, besides establishing mechanisms of social insurance for unemployment, the state also took responsibility for old age and inability to work, codified the principles of minimum wage and maximum work hours, and oversaw the regulation of child labor. Such issues, along with the level of wages and the size of the overall wage bill, were constitutive of the new norms of the reproduction of labor power. They therefore now fell within the remit of the state's direct responsibility to adapt the reproduction of labor power to the modalities and rhythms of the production of goods.

The terrain of struggle that preceded these new norms witnessed new subjects take the field: the unemployed, no longer a mere reserve army but rather a recomposed mass in struggle; workers who occupied factories and gained a powerful trade union; women, who in some cases gathered to organize themselves in a quasi-military fashion and who radically changed the reproductive organization of the working community.

Precisely for this reason, the need to ensure new reproductive conditions for labor power meant that the state also had to take responsibility for the distribution of mass wages. In other words, it had to distribute them rationally in view of development planning. At the same time, it had to try to establish a mechanism to regulate class struggle. A wage raise had to guarantee the worker's interest in development just as the unemployment allowance had to put an unemployed worker "into reserve," thereby keeping them off the streets. The family had to guarantee the actual wage capacity, and the continuous reproduction of labor power, by contributing itself to keeping the unemployed "in reserve" and supporting the disabled and the elderly. In the distribution-rationalization of the occupational possibilities that emerged from Roosevelt's New Deal, it is not by chance that the destiny of the female labor force remained substantially tied to the levels already established.

It would not be consistent with such rationality to promote women's employment, as it contrasted with the fact that women, as both government and trade unions desired, had to remain the main, indeed exclusive, figures responsible for ensuring the proper functioning of the family. As we have seen, this remained strongly evident, especially for married women who also worked outside the home.

The family remained the fundamental premise, not only to render the working class "organized" in the function of relaunching production, but also to more precisely adapt the entire social fabric to the possibility of capitalist planning. It is no coincidence that so many studies on the family and women, whether governmental or academic, reflect the desire of the system to place the family and the woman at the center of social organization and control over labor power.

96

APPENDIX

ON WELFARE

I thought I would use my reading of the editorial that appeared in *Primo Maggio 6*, along with an article titled "From March to November: A Critical Update," to briefly outline some ideas on the theme of welfare that have been introduced into Italy within the remit of the debate on public spending. While the following article is only meant to flag some important points, it is nonetheless more urgent than ever to clear up some matters. Indeed, an incorrect interpretation of welfare means an incorrect interpretation of class and of the relationship between class and capital today, including the infamous risk of arriving at conclusions that are substantially defeatist, in relation to which even scrap metal collecting, refused by the working class for many years now, might seem justified.

The first thing to say is that we continue to talk about welfare without seeing that those receiving it are, on a mass level, women. The figures speak clearly enough: in the United States, 85 percent of recipients are women, generally mothers with dependent children (Aid for Dependent Children). As concerns Supplemental Security Income (SSI), which is designed for the sick and elderly, and which up to 1975 was part of the welfare system, before being subsumed within Social Security (SS), the largest percentage is again constituted by women, comprised of housewives who have no pensions because 'they have never worked,' that is, they have never had a wage for a long enough period to allow them to access a social pension.

On the other hand, as to the processes of struggle that led to the current situation, so misunderstood by historians here in Italy, it should be enough to simply take a glance at the photos from the welfare movement that exploded in the United States in the 1960s, essentially a movement of women—black women—who knew how to provide a strategic outlet for the subversive energies of the youth. Young people burned the cities and carried out acts of mass appropriation—an outlet capable of establishing lasting power: a mass request for money that, inasmuch as it was made by those without wages, constituted a new mass power of the class. Spearheaded by women, the welfare movement was at the same time a wage demand and a rejection of the intensification of work, as they refused to take on a second job, instead demanding 'wages for housework.'

The perspective of the women who led these struggles is clearly expressed by statements like:

"The mother of a family already works full time at home, she doesn't need a second job."

"When there's a war the state suddenly remembers that they own our sons [it was the era of the Vietnam War]. Okay, so now they should pay us for how much it cost to raise them."

"Welfare isn't charity like the state wants us to think, it's our right, because we've already worked for this money."[1]

However, in the editorial and article mentioned at the outset, the focus is laid not so much on women but on unemployed whites or, more usually, black and Puerto Rican youth. In the author's mind, this is clearly a male proletariat, a fact that can be noted from the definition of welfare as 'income without work':

The politics of welfare derives from an idea of generalized public assistance, from an explicit assumption of the necessity for a certain level of unemployment in order to be able to effectively control social processes (marginalization, ghettoization, urban conflict, etc.). What brought this about was the continuous restructuring of the productive apparatus and, therefore of class composition.[2]

On the one hand, there was the strength of Black and Puerto Rican communities that Nixon was trying so hard to break, as well as attempting to undermine the direct relationship between the increase in factory struggles and the possibility of earning outside of the productive relation.[3]

In a version similar to the one already cited, those allusions to "*the welfare mothers* who Gisela Bock speaks about" are simply grotesques.[4] The women are rendered invisible, as is their labor and their struggle against it—and so is their first mass victory regarding wages for housework.

As well as this lack of recognition of welfare's 'political subjects,' there is also a distorted reading of the 'crisis,' one that is irrevocably bound to the discourse on welfare as the most significant sector in public spending. The problem is that the popular interpretation of the crisis in general (and the bankrupting of New York in particular), as one that is derived from the imbalance between productive and nonproductive sectors, says nothing about the basis that determined this crisis and the actual processes of class recomposition.

To be blind to the women on welfare is to be blind to the struggle over reproductive work as the determinative struggle regarding the very processes behind the crisis itself. The striking events of their indiscipline and refusal of work derived directly from the refusal of domestic work in the home, the office, the school, the nursery, and the factory. Furthermore, in relation to the elephantiasis of the public purse, it is nothing other than the state's desperate attempt—in the context of a *scaling up of refusal*—to continually *reconstruct and scale up* the *collective wife and mother,* who might once again discipline the workforce and persuade it to work. To be blind to all this is to fail to interpret the *necessity of growing imbalances* in state investment in public spending and to fixate on a void, providing a definition of the crisis that remains no more than descriptive, such as:

> The available information tells us that the New York bankruptcy, as in many American cities, resulted from

99

the huge increase in public spending, above all on welfare and on the growing bank debt . . . . From these two pieces of information one can agree with what so many have been saying, that is, that the current crisis everywhere is the result of an imbalance between the 'productive' and 'nonproductive' sectors.[5]

100

From 1965 onward, the welfare sector began to explode, both in terms of the number of recipients and of the kind of voices[6] through which the state forced the struggle to be expressed. That this was a women's struggle can be seen from the fact that it was precisely the category of the Aid for Dependent Children (AFDC) that exploded, while other categories[7] remained, on the whole, stagnant.[8] The other fact that has escaped Italian historians is that for the first time in the history of welfare the increase in the number of people receiving it was inversely proportional to unemployment. In fact, as Moynihan has already shown with some concern in his *The Politics of a Guaranteed Income*, the explosion in welfare was triggered in a period of mass economic expansion in the United States. For the first time, the relation between unemployment and welfare was completely broken.[9] This breakdown continued from 1966 until 1970, the year in which all American newspapers were in agreement that welfare was the 'national crisis' and that the situation 'was only getting worse.'

But what really was this national crisis that from 1970 onward became the thorn in the side of the American state?

The symbol of welfare dependence was the family with a mother at its head. Their continually growing number, to the point that in 1969 the *New York Daily News* reported— with neither anger nor disapproval but simply as a fact— "There is a quiet social revolution establishing itself in the country's slums, especially here in New York: the number of cases of absent fathers and illegitimate children is exploding, at the cost of the traditional family itself."[10]

Furthermore, Moynihan writes:

> The social fabric here in New York is falling to pieces . .
> . . For an ever-larger part of the population, the sense of
> discipline, of doing it oneself, of industry is slipping away
> . . . . The number of illegitimate children is growing; the
> family is ever more atomized and in the hands of women
> alone; crime and disorder are starkly increasing.... In
> short, we are seeing a growing disintegration of society.[11]

101

Ever since his famous report on the black family, Moynihan
has claimed that the origins of the ghetto revolts lay in the
fact that the majority of black families are led by women:
having no other authority over themselves, they rejected
their function of disciplining their children. In the article
"America," again from 1965, Moynihan writes:

> From the wilds of Irish slums of the Eastern seaboard,
> to the riot-torn suburbs of Los Angeles, there is one
> unmistakable lesson in American history: a community
> that allows a large number of young men to grow up in
> broken families, dominated by women, never acquiring
> any stable relationship to male authority, never acquir-
> ing any set of rational expectations about the future—
> that community asks for and gets chaos. Crime, violence,
> unrest, disorder—most particularly the furious, unre-
> strained lashing out at the whole social structure—that
> is not only to be expected; it is very near to inevitable.
> And it is richly deserved.

Even in today's debates about restructuring welfare,
Moynihan continues to repeat the fact that giving money
to women means undermining the family structure, and
thus the entire structure of work. That welfare might
function "not so much to bring stability but independence and consequentially the possibility of creating
entirely different family relations"[12]—and this, we must
understand, begins above all with women—is a fact about
which we have no doubts whatsoever. As all of the gov-

ernment documents from 1965 up till today verify, the explosion in welfare was concurrent with drastic increases in: 1) the number of so-called illegitimate children (this year in Washington, for the first time the number of illegitimate children overtook the number of legitimate ones); 2) the number of divorces, a figure that breaks new records every year. Furthermore, it is no longer the case that women who get divorced are childless.[13] All of this means a continual increase in the number of families with women at the head: between 1960 and 1970, an increase of 16 percent.

The *scaling up* of public spending, as I have already briefly mentioned above, was an act *forced on the American state by women's refusal of reproductive work*. The victory of the women over welfare—and in this sense, welfare is indeed the most important sector—has allowed for the generalization of this refusal. This is a refusal that has had the ability to move ever larger and more articulated investments into the sector of the social reproduction of the workforce. One really needs to be very blinkered in order not to see that the creation of the so-called 'third sector' is simultaneously a process of socialization of domestic work. Psychologists, sociologists, sexologists, teachers, social workers, therapists, doctors and nurses, etc. all have to perform the tasks that women increasingly refuse to undertake; all of them, to be precise, have to become the *collective wife* and mother. It is only in the light of this fact that one can understand why "service workers have had the lion's share."[14]

It was exactly in order to move toward a socialization of domestic work that the famous Title 20 (an amendment of the Social Security Act) was passed in 1975. It ensured the organization of a system of social services planned by the various states but, in the end, financed for the most part by the federal government, which created a new and mobile institution across the country that was destined to furnish domestic work, with the quite clear aim of controlling it. This included home services for the elderly and husbands with wives who were unable to perform domestic work and the provision of 'care' and 'alternative arrangements' for children growing up in 'inappropriate' housing, etc.

However, not even provisions like Title 20 managed to deal with the situation. Instead, the refusal only increased, taking on a mass character, producing a striking indiscipline from the home to the factory, a refusal of production and of being governed in any way, rendering the problem of public spending increasingly dramatic— not only for its fiscal aspect, though this was increasingly relevant, but also for its substantial endurance. By now, as capital knows all too well—even if some of its scholars are a little less clear—there is a quite precise connection between the *kitchen blues* and the *blue-collar blues*. In other words: the refusal in the kitchen means in turn an immediate refusal at the conveyor belt and in the army.[15] It is no accident that in mainstream newspapers like *Business Week* and *Magazine* women are blamed more and more for the explosion of struggles in schools, for the lack of victories in Vietnam, and for the clear lack of interest in working in general, as well as for the ever rising 'delinquency.'

However, the state knows it does not have adequate political instruments to deal with this problem. Investment in public spending is increasingly 'disproportionate' and 'expansive,' without there being any way to put the brakes on the situation, which has recently worsened because the new kind of human capital (social workers, etc.) in whom a large part of the public funds has been invested (and *had to be* invested), with no particular guarantee that this investment will not simply spiral out of control. The new agents who have to discipline those who have already refused the discipline are themselves undisciplined. As Peppino Ortoleva shows: "As far as the public service sector itself is concerned, those who administer the wide-ranging assistance, there are many recent examples of joint mobilizations that have included not only these workers but also 'their' recipients."[16] More specifically, focusing on the

103

ambit of welfare, which always remains the most significant, this unity in struggle between women recipients and
women social workers, who increasingly refuse to act as
police officers, is the most evident outcome of the refusal
of domestic work by both parties. It is precisely due to
the wave of this refusal that American capital has been
forced to attempt the path of a growing computerization
of welfare.[17]

The Nixon administration's counterattack began with
the apparent 'failure' of Johnson's 'Great Society' plan
(the realization of Kennedy's 'war on poverty'). This
counterattack took many forms, from the attempt to stop
the reproduction of the proletariat on welfare tout court
(from 1970 to today the sterilization of black and Puerto
Rican women, and those supported by welfare more generally, has increased threefold) to the cutting of welfare,
primarily through the elimination of the 'special needs'
category, and the introduction of the 'flat grant.' Overall,
there has been an attempt to reconnect welfare to the
male wage. Moynihan, always ahead of his times in this
regard, had by 1965 grasped that only the consolidation
of the economic position of the black male would solve
this spiral of indiscipline by the black proletariat. In this
sense the Nixon administration's Family Assistance Plan
(FAP) is the first program destined to explicitly reconstruct
the family, work, and masculine authority. Money will no
longer be directed to women but is to be attached to the
wage of the male worker to whom the woman and her
children are once again to bind themselves.[18] The FAP
has still not passed Senate, but it nonetheless shows the
general direction of all the proposed reforms that have
been and are currently being debated. This general direction remains the imperative of the discourse among the
more intelligent section of capital:

> The question isn't just about welfare but whether we'll
> give whole families the same economic help which we
> give to 'broken' ones today. Governor Car[e]y [of the

State of New York] has said that a system of welfare is
necessary to keep the family intact. But that's not what
we've got today. The current system provides a huge
incentive for families to break up. So that's the basic
issue: whether to give to the working poor [read: the
poor man] the same economic support which we give to
poor people on welfare. Everything else is simply administrative detail.[19]

There are others, however, who think instead that
the solution might lie in federalization, to the extent that
federalization represents first and foremost a wage cut[20]
but would also lead, with the centralization of welfare
management, to the elimination of local contracting and
therefore to the possibility for both the assisted and the
assistants to organize on a local level.[21]

In any case, even if everyone is in agreement on the
need for structural reform of welfare, this still hasn't
affected the process, precisely due to the 'difficulty' that
this presents.[22] A series of policies have been enacted,
however, that tend toward stabilizing masculine authority
within the family and, above all, to granting responsibility to the man for the maintenance of the children. It
will suffice to cite merely the most important of these
measures: the attempt to blackmail women by offering
economic compensation for officially providing the name
and address of their children's father;[23] macroscopically,
this attempt has failed—women know all too well that to
reconnect their children to the father also means to sub-
mit to his command—so more drastic means have been
tried. In April 1976, the federal government opened the
way to a kind of manhunt by allowing the Department for
Health, Education and Welfare (HEW) access to Social
Security numbers, thus granting them the ability to trace
fathers across state boundaries.[24] New York City went
further still: on February 16, 1977, it was decreed that
every woman who makes a welfare claim—the policy is
also retroactive—must declare who the father of the child

is, providing an address and any information that might allow him to be traced, as well as declaring "if at the time of conception she had relations with other men," as it is written in the new form that women have to fill out.

From the above it can be understood, therefore, that there is currently (and not only in the United States) an *unprecedented renewed interest by economists* in the *family* and that the *consolidation* of the family is today at *the center of the American government's politics*. It is no accident that the recent elections have brought Moynihan and Mondale to power (the latter the current vice president), the first being an expert on women and the second on children, and that Carter himself put praising the family at the center of his electoral campaign. We have already spoken about Moynihan at length. As far as Mondale is concerned, he introduced the Child and Family Services Act in 1975, which stated the *government's deep responsibility for the rearing of children*. There was hope that this Act would mean the allocation of federal funds for a vast range of projects for children in a range of states.[25] More recently, Mondale also asserted that every government plan ought be accompanied by a Family Impact Statement, so as to assess the influence that programs might have on family stability.

I have only spoken about the United States here. But insofar as the U.S. represents the country that leads capitalist reactions, we hope that this clarification might also provide some important indications about the dynamics of the 'world state' and of the class struggle over reproduction. We do so in the hope, as always, that those who are studying in order to contribute to the working-class debate do not, thereafter, in the great tradition of both the 'revolutionary' and the 'reformist' left, take an interest in simply rendering capital more intelligent.

Padua, April 1977

Originally published in *Primo Maggio: saggi e documenti per una storia di classe* 9–10 (1977–1978): 76–80.

NOTES

FOREWORD TO THE NEW EDITION

1. Lucía Cavallero and Verónica Gago, "Feminism, the Pandemic, and What Comes Next," *Critical Times: Interventions in Global Critical Theory*, April 21, 2020, https://ctjournal.org/2020/04/21/feminism-the-pandemic-and-what-comes-next.

PREFACE

2. M. Tronti, *Operai e Capitale* (Torino: Einaudi, 1966). See esp. 287ff.
3. AFDC is Aid to Families with Dependent Children.
4. See, for instance, two works on Argentina's social struggles that emphasize self-organization: Marina Sitrin, *Horizontalism: Voices of Popular Power in Argentina* (Oakland: AK Press, 2006); and Colectivo Situaciones, *19 & 20: Notes for a New Insurrection* (Brooklyn, NY: Common Notions 2021).

CHAPTER 1

1. For systemic issues relating to the Five-Dollar Day, see B. Coriat, *L'atelier et le chronomètre: Essai sur le taylorisme, le fordisme et la production de masse* (Bourgois: Paris, 1979), in particular chap. 4. See also: H. Beynon, *Working for Ford* (New York: Penguin Books, 1973) and A. Nevins, *Ford: the Times, the Man, the Company* (New York: Scribner, 1954). If 1914 was the year of Ford's famous proposal on wages, it should also be remembered that 1913 was the year of the introduction of the automatic assembly line. Owing to the new pressures this innovation posed to laborers, the rate of abandonment of the workplace by the workers was such that, as a close collaborator of Ford declared, "To add 100 workers to the factory staff, you had to take on 963." For this and other valuable information, see: P. Ortoleva, introduction to *La mia vita e la mia opera*, by H. Ford (Milan: La Salamandra, 1980), and P. Bairati, introduction to *Autobiografia*, by H. Ford, ed. S. Crowther (Milan: Biblioteca Universale Rizzoli, 1982).
2. Among reports that appeared in Italy, we should point out the numerous articles published in *Primo Maggio*: S. Tait, "Alle origini del movimento comunista negli Stati·Uniti: Louis Fraina teorico dell'azione di massa," B. Cartosio, "Note e documenti sugli Industrial Workers of the World," and G. Buonfino, "Il muschio non cresce sui sassi che rotolano: grafica e propaganda IWW," *Primo Maggio*, no. 1 (June–September 1973); P. Ortoleva, "Classe operaia e potere politico in Usa, 1860–1920," *Primo*

Maggio, nos. 3–4 (February–September 1974); Cartosio, "Storie e storici di operai americani," *Primo Maggio,* no. 11 (Winter 1977–78); Cartosio, "Mosca 1921: Una intervista a 'Big Bill' Haywood," which contains a) "Nostra intervista a Haywood Segret. Generale dell'IWW sulla situazione operaia negli Stati Uniti," and b) N. Vecchi, "Il pensiero di Haywood Segretario Generale dell'IWW sulla rivoluzione russa"; and S. Ghetti, "Gli IWW e la ristrutturazione del capitale negli anni venti," *Primo Maggio,* no. 16 (Fall–Winter 1981–82); Cartosio, "Gli emigrati italiani e l'IWW," *Primo Maggio,* no. 18 (Fall–Winter 1982–83). See also: P. Ortoleva, "Industrial Workers of the World," in P. Bairati ed., *Storia del Nord America,* Il mondo contemporaneo (Florence: La Nuova Italia, 1979), 147–156; G. Bock, P. Carpignano and B. Ramirez eds., *La formazione dell'operaio-massa negli USA: 1898–1922* (Milan: Feltrinelli, 1976); K. Allsop, *Hard Travellin': The Hobo and His History* (London: Hodder and Stoughton, 1967).

108

3. The industrialists themselves openly declared that they believed in the stability of the home as a response to the social instability of those years. "People should invest their savings in homes so that they become their own. That way they won't move and they won't go on strike" (cf. P. Carpignano, "Immigrazione e degradazione," in Bock, Carpignano and Ramirez, *La formazione dell'operaio-massa,* 221).

4. On the relationship between Fordism and family, see: G. Bock and B. Duden, "Arbeit aus Liebe, Liebe als Arbeit: Zur Entstehung der Hausarbeit im Kapitalismus," in Berliner Dozentinnengruppe ed., *Frauen und Wissenschaft* (Berlin: Courage Verlag, 1977); G. Bock, "L'altro movimento operaio negli Stati Uniti," and Carpignano, "Immigrazione e degradazione" (in particular, 218–221), in Bock, Carpignano and Ramirez, *La formazione dell'operaio-massa.* For some general observations on the relationship between deskilling of the labor force and family and social reproduction, see R.M. Titmuss, *Essays on "The Welfare State"* (Boston: Beacon Press, 1969), 104–118.

5. Cf. Coriat, *L'atelier et le chronomètre,* in particular chap. 4.

6. Ibid.

7. Sociologist J.R. Lee observes that five dollars a day in the hands of some men would be a serious handicap along the narrow path of righteousness, and would make them a potential threat to society. So, from the outset, it was settled that any man who was unable to use the wage with wisdom and prudence would not receive this raise. "The So-Called Profit Sharing System in the Ford Plant," *Annals of the Academy of Political Sciences,* vol. LXV (May 1916): 303.

8. "This double process—*ruin of the domestic balance and production on a capitalist basis of necessary goods*—is at the base of what will be indicated with the concept of new standards of worker consumption," says B. Coriat, *L'atelier*

et le chronomètre, who borrows the expression from M. Aglietta, *Régulation et crises du capitalisme* (Paris: Calmann-Lévy, 1977), 130. He continues, "In short, they mark the passage from the dominion of *not specifically mercantile conditions to precisely mercantile ones of reproduction of labor power*."

9. B. Ehrenreich and D. English, "The Manufacture of Housework," *Socialist Revolution*, no. 26 (October–December 1975): 6. Cf. A. Oakley, *Woman's Work* (New York: Vintage Books, 1976).

10. The most famous was Jane Addams. These middle-class women, who hoped to break free from the cult of domesticity through the work of *housekeepers of the nation*, helped to manage the Home Economics Movement. This movement, which developed after 1890, introduced new standards of "cleanliness, nutrition, family customs and efficiency in the kitchens primarily of the immigrant housewives, and measures and machines to save work in the kitchens of the wealthiest families, whose housekeepers preferred factory work to being personal house staff.... Making a science of the education of children was another highly promoted strategy. The militant feminist agitation for sex education, control and limitation of births, was reproached by the Socialists for producing a panic that would have caused women to lose all faith in men and to withdraw their capital—themselves—from the marriage market"; instead, on the side of capital, birth control could become a powerful instrument of state control over labor power. Bock, "L'altro movimento operaio negli Stati Uniti." On the relationship between feminism and socialism, see: M.J. Buhle, "Women and the Socialist Party, 1901–1914," in E.H. Altbach ed., *From Feminism to Liberation* (Cambridge, Mass.: Schenkman, 1971); B. Dancis, "Socialism and Women in the United States, 1900–1917," *Socialist Revolution* 27, vol. 6, no. 1 (January–March 1976); and M.J. Buhle, *Women and American Socialism, 1870–1920* (Urbana: University of Illinois Press, 1981). On domestic efficiency, see: M. Pattison, "Scientific Management in Home-Making," *Annals of the American Academy of Political and Social Science*, no. 48 (1913); and C. Perkins Gilman, *The Home: Its Work and Influence* (Urbana: University of Illinois Press, 1972), in particular chap. 5. Please note again, social workers came from that stratum of middle-class women who, by the turn of the century, had experienced a new degree of education and culture at a mass level. If the old productive functions were no longer needed, the new culture was still ghettoized in terms of "a ladies' sitting-room." Doing a job that was considered socially useful became a desirable outlet, even if it was almost always without pay, given that many women, in this vacuum of functions, were affected by hysteria and depression. Another outcome of the intellectual emancipation of women was the flourishing of women's associations that often applied themselves to social issues.

11. Cf. M. Tirabassi, "Prima le donne e i bambini; gli International Institutes e l'americanizzazione degli immigrati," the third article in the section entitled "Integrazione sociale negli Usa," edited by M. Vaudagna in *Quaderni storici*, no. 51, a. XVII, (December 1982): 853–880. The article is very interesting for its careful discussion of the role played by the International Institute.

12. W.C. Mitchell, "The Backward Art of Spending Money," *American Economic Review*, vol. II (June 1912): 269–281. Cf. A. Marshall, *Principles of Economics*, book VI, chap. IV (London: Macmillan, 1920). "The most valuable of all capital is that invested in human beings; and of that capital the most precious part is the result of the care and influence of the mother, so long as she retains her tender and unselfish instincts." In an analogous way, in the 1870s, articles appeared in *The New York Times* expressing concerns to dissuade women from claiming wages for their work: "If women wish the position of the wife to have the honor which they attach to it, they will not talk of the value of their services and about stated incomes, but they will live with their husbands in the spirit of the vow of the English marriage service, taking them 'for better, for worse, for richer, for poorer, in sickness and in health, to love, honor, obey.' This is to be a wife." "Wives' Wages," *The New York Times*, August 10, 1876. The quotation is from S. Federici's paper, "The Restructuring of Social Reproduction in the United States in the '70s," presented at the *Economic Policies of Female Labor in Italy and the United States* conference organized by the German Marshall Fund of the United States and the American Study Center, Rome, December 9–11, 1980. For a comparison with the positions expressed by the feminist movement at the time of the above-mentioned article's publication, see L. Gordon, *Woman's Body, Woman's Right: A Social History of Birth Control in America* (New York: Grossman, 1976).

13. For the different positions in the feminist movement, see: A.S. Kraditor, *The Ideas of the Woman Suffrage Movement: 1890–1920* (New York: Anchor Books, 1971), in particular 38ff.; D. Hayden, "Two Utopian Feminists and Their Campaigns for Kitchenless Houses," *Signs*, vol. 4, no. 2 (Winter 1978).

14. In 1908, the American Sociological Society conference was devoted to family problems and the ratification of divorce. If the claim of a more free sexuality was seen as a threat to the stability of the family, at that point even the most conservative forces warned that the only way to properly channel sexual tension was to permit a new flexibility to the institution of the family itself, and therefore, afford a new mobility to its members. Birth control also had to be accepted. At the time, divorce spread rapidly, the average age of marriage went up, and there was widespread practice of birth control. On the issues of divorce and

110

family problems at the time, see: W. O'Neill, *Divorce in the Progressive Era* (New Haven: Yale University Press, 1967); E. Shorther, *The Making of the Modern Family* (New York: Basic Books, 1977); and A. Calhoun, *A Social History of American Family* (New York: Barnes & Noble, 1960).

15. At the start of the 1900s, this issue marked the position of Crystal Eastman, a socialist feminist, who argued that "women who want to work in the home, or need to, should be paid for such work." "Now We Can Begin," in B. Wiesen Cook ed., *Crystal Eastman: On Women and Revolution* (Oxford: Oxford University Press, 1978). Crystal Eastman wrote that the only way for women in capitalist society to achieve real economic independence was for the government to recognize domestic labor as skilled labor and pay for it as such. Between 1903 and 1911, Eastman worked with people who shared this political position. However, it was not until the 1970s that "wages for housework" became an international claim upon which all components of the feminist movement debated and adopted a position. For some comments on this debate, see E. Malos, "Housework and the Politics of Women's Liberation," *Socialist Review* 37 (January–February 1978). For some indication of what appeared in the U.S. with respect to this debate, see *Radical America*, vol. 7, nos. 4–5 (July–October 1973): 131–192. This issue documents how the discussion was configured in Italy, the UK and the U.S. in the 1970s. For more recent studies, see N.J. Sokoloff, *Between Money and Love: The Dialectics of Women's Home and Market Work* (New York: Praeger Publishers, 1980), in particular chap. 4.

16. The quotation is from E. Flexner, *Century of Struggle: The Women's Rights Movement in the United States* (Cambridge: Belknap Press, 1959).

17. J.H. Spring, *Education and the Rise of the Corporate State* (Boston: Beacon Press, 1972), 78.

18. Ibid., 77–79.

19. Bock and Duden, "Arbeit aus Liebe."

20. Pure Food and Drug Act, 1906.

21. Carpignano, "Immigrazione e degradazione," underlines how, before trying to plan class dynamics (starting with the New Deal, and in the wake of the full development of the struggles of the mass worker), capital had to present itself as one of the terms of this institutional relationship. He cites R. Hofstadter, *The Age of Reform: From Bryan to F.D. Roosevelt* (New York: Knopf, 1955), 163, who says that Progressivism was a movement in which the aim was not that of a marked change in social structure but rather the formation of a responsible elite. See also: R. Hofstadter, *The Progressive Movement, 1900–1915* (Englewood Cliffs: Prentice Hall, 1963); J.R. Commons, *History of Labor in the United States, 1896–1932*, vols. III and IV (New York: Macmillan, 1935); Philip S. Foner, *History of the Labor Movement in the United States*, vol. III (New York: International Publishers, 1964);

111

Bairati ed., *Storia del Nord America*. For information that strictly pertains to the themes discussed here, see the following chapters: A.M. Martellone, "Immigrazione," 113–130, "Melting Pot," 198–203; P. Ortoleva, "Industrial Workers of the World", 147–156; A. Testi, "Progressive Era," 348–367; B. Cartosio, "Movimento operaio," 204–236.

22. It is appropriate to note that the law on the prohibition of alcohol in the United States, dating back to 1920, serves as a function of repression, especially against immigrants and Black people. It also aimed to destroy the saloon as a site of political unrest. Cf. K. Allsop, *The Bootleggers: The Story of Chicago's Prohibition Era* (London: Hutchinson and Co., 1961).

23. Don D. Lescohier, *The Labor Market* (New York: Macmillan, 1919), 255. Also cited in Carpignano, "Immigrazione e degradazione," 113.

24. *The Extent and Nature of So-Called Second Generation Problem*, IIB, box 23, quoted in Tirabassi, "Prima le donne e i bambini," 870.

25. As evidenced in A. Lorini, *Ingegneria umana e scienze sociali negli USA, 1890–1920* (Messina-Florence: D'Anna, 1980).

26. On the history of waged domestic labor and the changes of duties in relation to modernization, industrialization, and urbanization, see D.M. Katzman, *Seven Days a Week, Women and Domestic Service in Industrializing America* (New York and Oxford: Oxford University Press, 1978).

27. R. Schwartz Cowan, "The 'Industrial Revolution' in the Home: Household Technology and Social Change in the 20th Century," *Technology and Culture*, vol. 17, no. 1 (January 1976). The author maintains that the so-called industrial revolution in the home began in the middle-class kitchen as an attempt to save waged domestic work, and not in the kitchen of women who worked in the house and in the factory, contrary to the functionalist theory in sociology.

28. For the innovations mentioned above, see Cowan, "The 'Industrial Revolution' in the Home." A classic on the subject remains S. Giedion, *Mechanization Takes Command* (Oxford: Oxford University Press, 1948). Cf. also Douglass C. North, *Growth and Welfare in the American Past: A New Economic History* (Englewood Cliffs, NJ: Prentice Hall, 1966).

29. On the political ideology of consumption, cf. S. Ewen, "The Political Ideology of Consumption," presented at the *URPE Conference on Marxist Approaches to History*, Yale University, New Haven, February 24, 1974. Cf. also J. Hoff Wilson, *The Twenties: The Critical Issues* (New York: Little Brown & Co., 1972). Here Wilson argues that there were many consequences of this uneven prosperity. For example, those who did not experience it were frustrated because this was the decade in which mass consumption, or "consumerism," with all its kinds of publicity stunts and installment payments, became a basic feature of American life. The myriad of items which appeared for the first time after the First World War changed the buying habits of citizens belonging to the prosperous middle class (p. XIX).

See also G. Turnaturi, "La donna fra il pubblico e il privato: la nascita della casalinga e della consumatrice," *DWF*, nos. 12–13 (July–December 1979). Cf. also A.D. Gordon, M.J. Buhle, N.E. Schrom, "Women in American Society: A Historical Contribution," *Radical America*, vol. V, no. 4 (July–August 1971), 2nd ed. expanded as a brochure of *Radical America*, 1972.

30. On this widening of the tasks of the housewife, cf. Shorter, *Making of the Modern Family*, and R. Smuts, *Women and Work in America* (New York: Schocken Books, 1974). On the new complexities of marriage, see G.E. Hamilton and K. McGowan, *What is Wrong with Marriage* (New York: Boni, 1929).

31. For an analysis of the exchange that takes place in the marriage contract as a "labor of love," see G.F. Dalla Costa, *Un lavoro d'amore* (Rome: Edizioni delle Donne, 1978), in particular chap. 1. [Eng. tr., *The Work of Love* (Brooklyn: Autonomedia, 2008).] Cf. also Mariarosa Dalla Costa and Selma James, *Potere femminile e sovversione sociale* (Padua and Venice: Marsilio, 1972). [Eng. tr., *The Power of Women and the Subversion of the Community* (Bristol: Falling Wall Press, 1972).] For texts that analyze domestic work, the woman as its subject and the family as a place of production and reproduction of labor power rather than just consumption, see: S. Federici, *Wages against Housework* (New York: Power of Women Collective and Falling Wall Press, 1975), and S. Federici and N. Cox, *Counterplanning from the Kitchen* (New York: New York Wages for Housework Committee and Falling Wall Press, 1975), republished in *Revolution at Point Zero* (Oakland: Common Notions/ PM Press, 2012). Additionally, valuable explanations concerning the subsumption of sexual tasks in domestic work are contained in the following texts: S. Federici, *Sexual Work and the Struggle Against It* (unpublished work, New York, 1975); L. Fortunati, *L'arcano della riproduzione. Casalinghe, prostitute, operai e capital* (Venice: Marsilio, 1981). [Eng. tr., *The Arcane of Reproduction: Housework, Prostitution, Labor and Capital* (Brooklyn: Autonomedia, 1995).]

32. One can see a significant change in the advertising of products for the home in *Ladies Home Journal*. For example, before World War I the mistress of the house was usually shown with the maid, whereas after the war, only the mistress appeared, who "had to" use this or that product herself "for the sake of her loved ones." Both *Ladies Home Journal* and *Good Housekeeping* became principle promoters of Taylorism in the home.

33. See B. Ehrenreich and D. English, *For Her Own Good* (New York: Anchor Press, 1978). The authors devote a chapter to the germ theory that was born in the period we are examining. It was believed that dust contained germs that were the source of many serious diseases including tuberculosis. Furthermore, the authors designate the new figure of the housewife as "white collar" because she was called on to professionalize her work in a continuing symbiosis of intellectual and manual labor.

34. See J.R. Gillis, *Youth and History* (New York: Academic Press, 1974), particularly chap. 4.

35. Some interesting observations on the relationship between political repression and democracy of consumption are contained in B. Cartosio, "L'ingranaggio operaio nella macchina cinema," in *Tute e technicolor* (Milan: Feltrinelli, 1980).

36. To understand the meaning of the pin-money worker, for which there is no relative expression in Italian, one must keep in mind that the pin was what women at the time commonly used to affix a hat or adorn a garment. This phrase is meant to indicate the woman who works to satisfy her personal needs for luxury items rather than the bare necessities or family needs. It is therefore an expression marked by more of a selfish sense than the Italian expression "to work for extras," which might include a sense of satisfying family needs, even if not the bare necessities.

37. Cf. for the above data and additional information: D. Yoder, *Labor Economics and Labor Problems* (New York: McGraw-Hill Book Company, [1933] 1939), 347ff.; W.H. Chafe, *The American Woman: Her Changing Social, Economic and Politcal Roles, 1920–1970* (Oxford, New York, London: Oxford University Press, [1972] 1974); W.D. Wandersee, *Women's Work and Family Values, 1920–1940* (Cambridge and London: Harvard University Press, 1981), 89ff.; L. Wolman, *The Growth of American Trade Unions, 1880–1923*, Publications of the National Bureau of Economic Research, no. 6 (New York, 1924), 100–104.

38. For further comments on the most salient moments of struggle in these two periods, see chap. 2.

39. I.M. Rubinow, *Social Insurance: With Special Reference to American Conditions* (New York: H. Holt and Co., 1913), 435–436, cited in R. Lubove, *The Struggle for Social Security, 1900–1935* (Cambridge, Mass.: Harvard University Press, 1968), 91. In recent years, some works, starting from the study of J. Weinstein, *The Corporate Ideal in the Liberal State* (Boston: Beacon Press, 1968), have analyzed several of the first legislative actions of the early 1900s on social insurance in view of so-called "Corporate Liberalism." Social welfare legislation (e.g., legislation on workmen's compensation) was thus seen as one of the instruments adopted by big business to ensure the most efficient and fluid functioning possible of the capitalist economy.

40. The BPW began its existence in Kansas City in 1908 when its City Hall established a Board of Pardons and Paroles among the guests of the workhouse. The following year it became the administrator of the workhouse itself. In 1910, its functions were extended to include the duties of the city for all the poor, criminals, unemployed, unfortunate and abandoned classes in the community, and to oversee private agencies that raised funds from the public for these purposes. L.A. Halbert, "Board of Public Welfare; A System of Government Social Work," National Conference of Social Work, *Proceedings* (1918), 220–221, cited in Lubove, *The Struggle for Social Security*, 94. Within a few years, the BPW was extended to many other cities.

41. T. Roosevelt, "Special Message to Congress, February 15, 1909", *Proceedings of the Conference on the Care of Dependent Children*, Washington, DC, January 25–26, 1909.

42. Ibid.

43. Bock and Duden, "Arbeit aus Liebe."

CHAPTER 2

1. M. Gobbini, "La tavola rotonda alla Norman Wait Harris Foundation," in Gobbini ed., *J.M. Keynes, Inediti sulla crisi* (Rome: Istituto dell'Enciclopedia Italiana, 1976), 44. For advanced political readings of the debate in Italy on the crisis of 1929 and the 1930s, see: A. Negri, "La teoria capitalistica del '29: John M. Keynes," *Contropiano*, no. 1 (1968): 3–40; M. Tronti, "Classe operaia e sviluppo," *Contropiano*, no. 3 (1970): 465–477; S. Bologna et al., *Operai e stato* (Milan: Feltrinelli, 1972). For an interpretation of the crisis, see: C.P. Kindleberger, *The World in Depression, 1929–1939* (London: Allen Lane, The Penguin Press, 1973); as well as his "Crisi del 1929," in Bairati ed., *Storia del Nord America*, 46–62.

2. A.M. Schlesinger Jr., *The Age of Roosevelt*, vol. II, *The Coming of the New Deal* (Boston: Houghton Mifflin Company, 1959), 263, estimates that there were 12 to 15 million people unemployed (more than a quarter of all American workers) on the day that Roosevelt entered office.

3. Gobbini, "La tavola rotonda," 50.

4. D. Guerin, *Il movimento operaio negli Stati Uniti*, trans. M. Maggi (Rome: Editori Riuniti, 1975), 75.

5. I. Bernstein, *The Lean Years: A History of the American Worker, 1920–1933* (Boston: Houghton Mifflin Co., 1972), 54, 251.

6. A.M. Schlesinger Jr., *The Age of Roosevelt*, vol. I, *The Crisis of the Old Order, 1919–1933* (Boston: Houghton Mifflin Co., 1957), 67.

7. *Ibid.*, 105.

8. Guerin, *Il movimento operaio negli Stati Uniti*, 64.

9. Ibid.

10. Cf., for the standpoint of the courts: E. Faulkner Baker, *Technology and Woman's Work* (New York: Columbia University Press, 1964), in particular, chap. 21, Part V on protective legislation toward women. "Estimates of minimum 'health-and-decency' budgets ran from $1,820 to $2,080 a year; but average earnings of workers never rose above $1,500 at any point in the decade. And there were many below the average. In 1922 the average hourly wage for a male weaver in Alabama was 25 cents, for a female frame spinner, 17 cents. Nor could it be said that labor was paid off in increased leisure. The average work week remained around 50 hours, and in some industries it was longer. Even at the end of the decade, tens of thousands of steelworkers were working seven days a week and thousands were working 84 hours.

In southern textile mills, women and children worked from 54 to 60 or 70 hours a week. And business leaders were generally hostile to proposals for a five-day week. 'Nothing breeds radicalism more quickly than unhappiness unless it is leisure,' said the president of the National Association of Manufacturers in 1929." Schlesinger, *The Age of Roosevelt*, vol. I, 111–112.

11. William Z. Foster and Elisabeth G. Flynn were two members of the IWW under whose leadership the steel workers, divided into numerous small craft unions, sought to overcome the organizational limitations of this kind of union. The steel sector was hit particularly hard during the war by the rationalization of production. Foster and Flynn would become leaders of the recently formed Communist Party. See E.G. Flynn, *The Rebel Girl: An Autobiography, My First Life, 1906–1926* (New York: International Publishers Co., 1973). On the strike of 1919, see C.E. Warne ed., *The Steel Strike of 1919: Problems in American Civilization* (Boston: D.C. Heath and Co., 1963).

12. G.P. Rawick, "Anni venti: lotte operaie USA," in Bologna et al., *Operai e stato*, provides details of strikes in Loray, Tennessee, in Danville and Gastonia, North Carolina, and in Passaic, New Jersey, places where the Communist Party was able to play an important role because the AFL was not inclined to try unionizing underqualified workers in backward areas. If sectors such as textiles, clothing, and less expensive consumer goods employed predominantly white male workers in the South, in the North they employed women. On the relationship between women and unions, see Alice Henry, *The Trade Union Woman* (New York and London: D. Appleton and Co., 1915) and *Women and the Labor Movement* (New York: George H. Doran Co., 1923). On the relationship between the feminist movement and women workers, see: A.S. Kraditor, *The Ideas of the Woman Suffrage Movement: 1890–1920*; Kraditor ed., *Up from the Pedestal: Selected Writings in the History of American Feminism* (Chicago: Quadrangle Books, 1968); W. O'Neill, *Everyone was Brave: A History of Feminism in America* (Chicago: Quadrangle Books, 1971); H. Marot, *American Labor Unions, by a Member* (New York: H. Holt and Co., 1915). On the factory experience of the early decades of the twentieth century, well documented by women workers, social reformers, and middle-class women who were interested in the matter, see: D. Richardson, *The Long Day: The Story of a New York Working Girl as Told by Herself* (New York: The Century Co., 1905); E. Dean Bullock, *Selected Articles on the Employment of Women* (Minneapolis: The H.W. Wilson Co., 1911); G. Hughes, *Mothers in Industry: Wage Earning by Mothers in Philadelphia* (New York: New Republic Inc., 1925). For the experience of social workers in particular, see A. Davis, *Spearheads of Reform* (New York: Oxford University Press, 1967). For a view of women's employment, J. Hill, *Women in Gainful Occupations, 1870–1920: A Study of the Trend* (Washington, DC: U.S. Government Printing Office, 1929).

13. Here, the Women's Trade Union League was moving together with the International Ladies' Garment Workers' Union, whose base often clashed with a management group allied with the AFL bureaucracy. For a history of the WTUL, see G. Boone, *The Women's Trade Union Leagues in Great Britain and in the United States of America* (New York: AMS Press, 1968). For struggles involving the conditions of all the above-mentioned categories of female workers, see ibid. For a history of developments in women's wages in industry, up to just before the 1920s, see E. J. Hutchinson, *Women's Wages: A Study of the Wages of Industrial Women and Measures Suggested to Increase Them* (New York: AMS Press, 1968). Baker, *Technology and Woman's Work*, informs us that the first minimum wage laws were enacted for all male and female sweatshop workers in New Zealand, Australia, Great Britain and then, for the first time in the USA, in Massachusetts in 1912. It was, in this case, a nonmandatory law on the minimum wage for women, which depended purely on public opinion for its application. There was a big collaboration between the Consumers' Leagues and the WTUL to support it and similar laws were passed in other states. Some, however, were annulled. The judiciary, referring to the recent enactment of the 9th Amendment granting women the vote, cited that since women had become equal there was no longer need to protect them. During the 1920s many of these laws were declared unconstitutional.

14. In fact, such laws would have limited the freedom of contract of the parties involved, which, according to the judiciary, expressed a communist spirit. Cf. Boone, *The Women's Trade Union Leagues.*

15. Ibid. See also Yoder, *Labor Economics and Labor Problems.*

16. The Women's Bureau, "Industrial Homework," *Bulletin*, no. 79 (Washington, 1930), indicates fixing buttons, hook closures and safety pins on cardboard, sewing garters, manufacture of jewelery, lamps, powder puffs, and rag rugs as work to be carried out at home, among many other tasks.

17. Cf. Yoder, *Labor Economics and Labor Problems*, 365ff. In 1936, nine states had laws on work at home. By 1939, the number had risen to twenty-four states. Legislative slowness was based, among other things, on the reluctance of the courts to "allow the law to invade the homes of citizens" (370). In the same text, on 367, see the interesting table comparing the performance of work at home and employment in industry for the years 1911–1930. Cf. also S.M. Soffee, "Industrial Housework in Pennsylvania," *American Federationist*, vol. 36, no. 9 (September 1929): 1062–1063.

18. Boone, *The Women's Trade Union Leagues*, 114ff. The author also emphasizes the collaborative relationship with the General Federation of Women's Clubs. In 1908 the League of Chicago (or Illinois League) urged the governor to provide legislation that would limit the work day to eight hours and for the establishment of a commission to inves-

117

tigate work at home. In 1918 the collaboration between the Leagues of women, consumers, the General Federation of Women's Clubs and the YWCA led to the establishment of the Women in Industry Service within the Department of Labor (founded in 1912), which in 1920 was recognized as a Division under the name of Women's Bureau. It is also worth remembering that the Worker's Education Bureau was also established in 1921. The safety problem had been raised for some time, primarily as a need for protection from fire. Many local leagues had called for measures in this regard. "In the spring of 1911 nearly 150 girls died in a fire at the Triangle Shirtwaist Factory, suffocating in the narrow space behind locked doors, or leaping, screaming, to the streets below. The disaster shocked the public into protest. A citizens' committee on safety was formed. . . . Frances Perkins, as an investigator for the Commission . . . made Bob Wagner crawl through the tiny hole in the wall, marked 'Fire Escape,' to the steep iron ladder covered with ice and ending twelve feet above the ground." Schlesinger, *The Age of Roosevelt*, vol. I, 96. Cf. also the speech by Rose Schneiderman in this regard in Boone, *The Women's Trade Union Leagues*, 189.

19. J.L. Davis, "Safeguarding the Mothers of Tomorrow," *Gazette of Colorado Springs*, November 5, 1922. More advisedly, at the national convention of the League in 1929, Rose Schneiderman said that the problem of women in the factory was growing complicated because women no longer seemed destined to stay there temporarily, and even married women seemed as if they were there to stay. See Boone, *The Women's Trade Union Leagues*, 188. Schneiderman thereby grasped that if capital, during the years immediately preceding, had held out to maintain female employment levels compressed at the given level, the entry of women into paid work had nevertheless initiated an irreversible process, and within it, married women have played a particularly important role.

20. Along with the destruction of the IWW movement, implemented mostly during the war, one cannot help but recall, amidst the fierce attack on the immigrant community, the story of Sacco and Vanzetti.

21. Woods "submitted to the President a draft message to Congress calling for a Public Works program, including slum clearance, low-cost housing and rural electrification. Woods and his Committee also favored Senator Robert F. Wagner's bills proposing the advance planning of public works and setting up a national employment service. But the President, rejecting the Woods program, addressed Congress with his usual optimism." Schlesinger, *The Age of Roosevelt*, vol. I, 170.

22. Bernstein, *The Lean Years*, 254, 256, 257.

23. It is well known that hundreds of small entrepreneurs committed suicide when their companies went bankrupt.

24. Schlesinger, *The Age of Roosevelt*, vol. I, 171.

118

25. "Citizens of Chicago ... could be seen digging into heaps of refuse with sticks and hands as soon as the garbage trucks pulled out." Ibid.

26. On the structure of the employment of Black people in the United States, the most comprehensive work is the series of monographs edited by the Industrial Research Unit, Wharton School of Finance and Commerce, *Studies of Negro Employment*, in more than 20 volumes, University of Pennsylvania Press, Philadelphia, published since 1968, and carried out largely under the guidance of R. Northrup. With World War I, several substantial groups of Black labor power entered into the mass production of large-scale industry, particularly in the automobile, meat and steel sectors. In particular, in the automobile sector the entrance of Black people came about in order to replace the white labor which quickly abandoned the monotony and the rhythms of the assembly line. At the same time, the need for capital to use Black labor came from not being able to draw on foreign labor, given the measures to block immigration.

27. The mass entrance of Black people in industry took place, as it did for women, with the Second World War. In 1942, the porters' union, led by A. Philip Randolph, posted a threat in the "Daily Worker," of a march on Washington if action wasn't taken against racial discrimination in recruitment in the war industries. Roosevelt then issued the famous federal order 8802 for the hiring of Black people in the industries of war materials, and the establishment of the Fair Employment Practices Commission became necessary. One should, however, keep in mind the continuity between Black people's ability to resist and struggle in the 1930s, as we shall see later, and their being able to assert themselves during the war.

28. There are numerous sociological studies aimed at measuring the effects of the crisis on family order. Just to name a few: Bernstein, *The Lean Years*; E.W. Bakke, *The Unemployed Man: A Social Study* (New York: E.P. Dutton and Co., 1934); R.A. Cooley, *The Family Encounters the Depression* (New York: Charles Scribner's Sons, 1936); S. Stouffer and P. Lazarsfeld, "Research Memorandum on the Family in the Depression," *Social Science Research Council Bulletin*, no. 29; M. Komarovsky, *The Unemployed Man and His Family: The Effect of Unemployment upon the Status of the Man in Fifty-nine Families* (New York: The Dryden Press Inc., 1940). An obvious classic is the two-volume work of R.S. Lynd and H.M. Lynd, *Middletown*, vol. I, and *Middletown in Transition: A Study in Cultural Conflicts*, vol. II (New York: Harcourt, Brace & World, 1929 and 1937). This survey remains one of the most famous sociological examinations of the impact of the Depression on a medium-sized city, first in 1925 (vol. I) and then in 1935 (vol. II). The authors devote particular attention to changes in family relationships. See also: A.E. Wood and J. Barker Waite, *Crime and Its Treatment: Social and Legal Aspects of Criminology*

(New York: American Book Co., 1941); M.A. Elliot and F.E. Merrill, *Social Disorganization* (New York: Harper and Brothers, 1936).

29. See Cesare Lombroso (with Gina Lombroso-Ferrero), *Criminal Man, According to the Classification of Cesare Lombroso* (New York: Putnam, [1911] 1975). One often cited pathological explanation for crime was precocious puberty. See Elliott and Merrill, *Social Disorganization*.

30. Elliott and Merrill, *Social Disorganization*, 100.

31. Schlesinger, *The Age of Roosevelt*, vol. I, 171.

32. In addition to the classics on the Great Depression, cf. particularly for the aspect of mobility of family order: C.C. Zimmerman and N.L. Whetten, *Rural Families on Relief* (New York: Capo Press Reprint Series, 1971); R.S. Cavan and K.H. Ranck, *The Family and the Depression: A Study of One Hundred Chicago Families* (New York: Arno Press and The New York Times, 1971); *Women Workers after a Plant Shutdown* (Harrisburg: Pennsylvania Department of Labor and Industry, Bureau of Women and Children, Special Bulletin, no. 26, 1933). It was reputed that in 1933, one third of the population, i.e., forty million men, women and children, were living without a regular source of income.

33. Schlesinger, *The Age of Roosevelt*, vol. I, 251: "They traveled on train bumpers or hitched rides from passing cars, they slept in homeless shelters in the cities or the railway stations. . . . For a moment, the two or three hundred thousand young people among them seemed the *bezprizorni* of America, the wild boys of the road."

34. Bernstein, *The Lean Years*, 325. On vagrant women, see B. Reitman, *Sister of the Road: The Autobiography of Boxcar Bertha* (New York: Harper and Row, 1975).

35. Schlesinger, *The Age of Roosevelt*, vol. I, 259.

36. Bernstein, *The Lean Years*, 328. See also the interviews conducted in Studs Terkel, *Hard Times: An Oral History of the Great Depression* (New York: Pantheon Books/Avon Books, 1970). What one woman says about the reasons that led to the decline of marriage is particularly interesting: "There were young men around when we were young. But they were supporting their mothers. It wasn't that we didn't have the chance. I was going with someone when the Depression hit. We probably would have gotten married. He was a commercial artist and had been doing very well. I remember the night he said, 'They just laid off quite a few of the boys.' It never occurred to him that he would be next. He was older than most of the others and very sure of himself. This was not the sort of thing that was going to happen to *him*. Suddenly he was laid off. It hit him like a ton of bricks. And he just disappeared." (447). In this regard, see also the considerations of Ruth Milkman, "Women's Work and the Economic Crisis," *Review of Radical Political Economics*, vol. 8, no. 1 (1976).

37. Bernstein, *The Lean Years*, 328, and Schlesinger, *The Age of Roosevelt*, vol. I,

251. For other considerations on the decline of births and their recovery after 1935, see John Philip Wernette, *Government and Business* (New York: The Macmillan Co., 1964).

38. Bernstein, *The Lean Years*, 328.

39. Schlesinger, *The Age of Roosevelt*, vol. I, 171.

40. Bernstein, *The Lean Years*, 325.

41. Elliott and Merrill, *Social Disorganization*, 170.

42. Cavan and Ranck, *Family and the Depression*, and Komarovsky, *Unemployed Man and His Family*.

43. Bernstein, *The Lean Years*, 331.

44. F. Fox Piven and R.A. Cloward, *Poor People's Movements: Why They Succeed, How They Fail* (New York: Vintage Books, 1979), 48.

45. Bernstein, *The Lean Years*, 327.

46. Ibid., 328; see also Milkman, "Women's Work and the Economic Crisis."

47. Ibid.

48. Bernstein, *The Lean Years*, 327–328.

49. Elliott and Merrill, *Social Disorganization*, 97ff. Cf. also Bernstein, *The Lean Years*, 422.

50. President's Research Committee on Social Trends, *Recent Social Trends in the United States* (New York: McGraw-Hill Books, 1933).

51. Elliott and Merrill estimate that for the youth who worked, the chances of breaking the law were quadrupled. See *Social Disorganization*, 100. Surveys conducted before 1934 show that 69 percent of imprisoned juveniles were newspaper sellers. See also Wood and Waite, *Crime and Its Treatment*, 159.

52. Elliott and Merrill, *Social Disorganization*, 87.

53. Ibid., 89.

54. Cf. also the comments made by Elliott and Merrill, *Social Disorganization*, 95ff.

55. E.F. Frazier, *The Negro Family in the United States* (New York: Dryden Press, 1951), 223. A fundamental text on the history of the Black family and the Black community in the United States, and notoriously at odds with the overall interpretation of Frazier, is H.G. Gutman, *The Black Family in Slavery and Freedom, 1750–1925* (New York: Vintage Books, 1977). Among the best studies translated into Italian is G.P. Rawick, *From Sundown to Sunup: The Making of the Black Community* (Westport, CT: Greenwood Publishing Co., 1972). For some testimonies of Black women in relation to the period we are considering, see G. Lerner ed., *Black Women in White America: A Documentary History* (New York: Vintage Books, 1973).

56. Rawick, *From Sundown to Sunup*, 157.

57. E.F. Frazier, *The Negro in the United States* (Toronto: Macmillan Co., 1957), 599. See also the following studies: R. Sterner, *The Negro's Share*, New

121

York, 1943; National Urban League, *Unemployment Status of Negroes: A Compilation of Facts and Figures Respecting Unemployment in One Hundred and Six Cities* (New York, 1931); and National Urban League, *The Forgotten Tenth: An Analysis of Unemployment Among Negroes in the United States and its Social Costs, 1932–33* (New York, 1933).

58. Cf. Frazier, *The Negro Family in the United States*, 217.

59. Ibid., 220.

60. Translator's note: The "Bright Lights District," and more generally, Chicago's South Side "Black Belt" was home to the city's African American population, as well as a vibrant Black Arts community during the peak of the Jazz Age in the 1920s.

61. Cf. Frazier, *The Negro in the United States*, 579.

62. Elliott and Merrill, *Social Disorganization*, 170.

63. Ibid., 577–579 and 581–583.

64. Frazier, *The Negro in the United States*, 577.

CHAPTER 3

1. For a history of aid to the unemployed before the Great Depression, see Lubove, *The Struggle for Social Security*, 144–180. The American Association of Labor Legislation (AALL) organized two national conferences in 1914 from which the "Practical Program" of 1914–15 emerged. While acknowledging that the problem could not be attributed to individual reasons or to the unwillingness to work, but that the phenomenon was inherent in the current method of social organization, the Program's solution proposed the following: a better distribution of jobs by agencies, the creation of apprenticeships and public works (with a warning not to let these become made-up posts for "assistants" etc.), techniques to make employment more stable and lower the turnover rate, the revival of agriculture, and other measures. The phenomenon of unemployment was essentially attributed to a market irrationality that could be overcome by distributing more equally the employment opportunities and the population according to these opportunities. The policy of emigration, claimed the AALL, had to be "constructive" for a more appropriate distribution of the enormous immigration in America. At the bottom of the list of proposals, with respect to individuals not recoverable through this total redistributive effort, there was, for the weak of mind, segregation, and for the poor professionals and semi-criminal elements, agricultural penal colonies.

2. Bernstein, *The Lean Years*, 328: "Women, particularly in the early years of the Depression, refused to believe that jobs were not to be had; something must be wrong with the man. 'Have you anybody you can send around . . . to tell my wife you have no job to give me?' an unemployed Philadelphian asked a social worker. 'She thinks I don't want to work.'"

3. See W.E. Leuchtenburg, "La grande depressione," in M. Vaudagna ed., *Il New Deal* (Bologna: Il Mulino, 1981), 317–318: "Not accustomed to adversity, Americans lived the Depression worse than other countries which had not enjoyed the economic boom of the 1920s.... The Depression represented a blow to American confidence in the uniqueness of its civilization."

4. R.O. Boyer and H.M. Morais, *Labor's Untold Story* (New York: United Electrical, Radio and Machine Workers of America, [1955] 1970), 250–251.

5. Ibid., 256, 259. The story goes on until the intervention of neighbors and the Unemployed Council to recover Mr. Grossup's furniture from the street because he had been evicted. "Mr. Grossup never knew how it all happened. It was a happy blur. He had his home again. He had strength. He had friends. . . . It was like a party. Everyone was shouting and laughing and Mr. Grossup shook hands with at least two-dozen men he had never met before. The Negro leader of the unemployed, Hugh Henderson, a sandwich in his hand, was making a speech from the front porch. Mr. Grossup somehow found himself making a speech too. . . . There were cheers. Some of the crowd went away but more seemed inside the house. . . . A great tension, and awful loneliness, was slowly seeping from Mr. Grossup's veins. He hadn't known how miserable he had been. A man couldn't do anything by himself. He hadn't known how many people had been going through the same things he had."

6. L. Adamic, *My America, 1928–1938* (New York: Harpers and Brothers, 1938), 309, in J. Brecher, *Strike!* (San Francisco: Straight Arrow Books, 1972), 144. This text provides useful information about the struggles of the unemployed and workers.

7. Bernstein, *The Lean Years*, 421–423.

8. P. Ortoleva, "'Republic of the Penniless': radicalismo politico e 'radicalismo sociale' tra i disoccupati americani, 1929–1933," *Rivista di storia contemporanea*, fasc. 3, a. X (July 1981): 387–416.

9. Brecher, *Strike!*, opens Chapter 5 on the struggles during the Depression with this slogan, 144. Some systematic considerations on the movement of the unemployed up to 1933 are contained in P. Ortoleva, "Il movimento dei disoccupati negli Usa (1930–1933)," *Primo Maggio*, no. 8 (Spring 1977).

10. Piven and Cloward, *Poor People's Movements*, devote a large commentary to the role played by Communists, Socialists, and Musteists, particularly in relation to the efforts for organization at a national level.

11. Bernstein, *The Lean Years*, 426–427.

12. Ibid., 427.

13. This amount would not be paid until 1945.

14. Schlesinger, *The Age of Roosevelt*, vol. I, 262. Cf. also Bernstein, *The Lean Years*, 453.

15. Schlesinger, *The Age of Roosevelt*, vol. II, 256.

16. Ibid., 241.

17. It should be recalled that until the late 1930s, hirings within the civil service were primarily regulated by the criteria of political clientele. With the federal request of 1939, the government sought instead to introduce meritocratic criteria and the principle of authority to prevent the formation of local powers that were outside the government's control.

18. We find a detailed account of this and other demonstrations that ended in bloodshed in H.D. Lasswell and D. Blumenstock, *World Revolutionary Propaganda* (Plainview: Books for Libraries Press, 1970). Chicago, in fact, had already been the site of frequent spontaneous outbursts, struggles against evictions, and other struggles. Not just in the period we are considering but also during the crisis of 1873 when 20,000 anarchists, chanting "bread or blood," marched on the headquarters of the city council. That same year, marches of 10,000 or 15,000 people also took place in New York City. See L.H. Feder, *Unemployment Relief in Periods of Depressions* (New York: Russel Sage Foundation, 1936).

19. A.M. Schlesinger Jr., *The Age of Roosevelt*, vol. III, *The Politics of Upheaval, 1935–1936* (Boston: Houghton Mifflin Company, 1960), 29. See also chap. 3 of this volume.

20. F. Fox Piven and R.A. Cloward, *Regulating the Poor: The Functions of Public Welfare* (New York: Vintage Books, 1971), 101, remains a classic text for information about the struggles during the Depression. Cf. A. Holtzman, *The Townsend Movement* (New York: Bookman, 1963).

21. Among the best books analyzing the various ideological positions of the New Deal period in the U.S. are two by R. Hofstadter: *The American Political Tradition and the Men Who Made It* (New York: Alfred A. Knopf, 1951), and *The Age of Reform: From Bryan to F.D. Roosevelt* (see chap. 1, n. 20).

22. Schlesinger, *The Age of Roosevelt*, vol. III, 42.

23. *The American Progress*, vol. I, no. 32 (March 29, 1934): 1, cited in B. Rauch, *The History of the New Deal, 1933–1938* (New York: Capricorn Books, 1963), 172. Cf. also T.H. William, *Huey Long* (New York: Alfred A. Knopf, 1970).

24. See C.J. Tull, *Father Coughlin and the New Deal* (Syracuse: Syracuse University Press, 1965). There is broad consensus on the ambiguity of this figure as well, who was known to be a self-declared anti-Semite.

25. R. Hofstadter and M. Wallace, *American Violence: A Documentary History* (New York: Vintage Books, 1971), 159. In 1932, when the Local Council organized groups of unemployed people who were breaking into agencies, in Harlem, 80% of heads of households were unemployed.

26. Piven and Cloward, *Poor People's Movements*, 53.

27. Ibid., 54–55. Cf. also Bernstein, *The Lean Years*, and Lasswell and Blumenstock, *World Revolutionary Propaganda*.

28. Boyer and Morais, *Labor's Untold Story*, 260.
29. Schlesinger, *The Age of Roosevelt*, vol. I, 251.
30. P. Ortoleva, "Republic of the Penniless," 401, 408, 410.
31. Ibid.
32. Brecher, *Strike!*, 146.
33. Ibid.
34. Ibid., 147.
35. Ibid.
36. Bernstein, *The Lean Years*, 322.
37. On the factory struggles, see the final chapter.

CHAPTER 4

1. Hofstadter, *The American Political Tradition*, 372–373.
2. Ibid., 390. See also: W.S. Myers ed., *The State Papers and Other Writings of Herbert Hoover*, 2 vols. (New York: Doubleday, 1934); and W.S. Myers and W.H. Newton eds., *The Hoover Administration: A Documented Narrative* (New York and London: Scribner's Sons, 1936).
3. Schlesinger, *The Age of Roosevelt*, vol. I, 169.
4. Ibid.
5. Hofstadter, *The American Political Tradition*. On 399, Hofstadter observes, "The peculiar economic theology that underlay Hoover's attitude toward relief was highlighted by the political aftermath of the 1930 drought. In December, Hoover approved a Congressional appropriation of 45 million dollars to save the livestock of stricken Arkansas farmers, but opposed an additional 25 million to feed the farmers and their families, insisting that the Red Cross could take care of them." Cf. also Schlesinger, *The Age of Roosevelt*, vol. I, 175.
6. Ibid. Cf. also Schlesinger, *The Age of Roosevelt*, vol. I, 184–185.
7. Schlesinger, *The Age of Roosevelt*, vol. 1, 178–179. At the same time he also claimed, in agreement with Hoover, that that social disorder, the real problem overshadowing all others "like a colossus," was not unemployment but crime. Ibid., 177.
8. Ibid., 176.
9. Cf. J. Pool and S. Pool, *Who Financed Hitler* (New York: Dial Press, 1979), 96.
10. Ibid., 181.
11. Ibid., 181.
12. Schlesinger, The Age of Roosevelt, vol. 1, 241. Cf. also G. Nash, "Herbert Hoover and the Origins of the Reconstruction Finance Corporation," *Mississippi Valley Historical Review* XLVI (December 1959).
13. Schlesinger, *The Age of Roosevelt*, vol. I, 236.
14. "The mass unemployment experienced during the inter-war period was of two main types. On the one hand, there was special, localized

(or 'structural') unemployment in industries which had been expanded during the war beyond the size required for peace-time conditions, or for which the demand had permanently shrunk as a result of technological, political, or other developments. . . . On the other hand, there was the general unemployment, connected with the trade cycle, which was not confined to particular industries but was spread throughout the economy and reflected a general deficiency of effective demand or deflation." See H.W. Arndt, *The Economic Lessons of the Nineteen-Thirties* (New York: Oxford University Press, 1949), 250–251.

126

15. The main source on F.D. Roosevelt is S.I. Rosenman ed., *The Public Papers and Addresses of Franklin Delano Roosevelt*, 13 vols. (New York: Random House, 1938–50), and by the same author, *Working with Roosevelt* (New York: Harper, 1952). See also: J.M. Burns, *Roosevelt: The Lion and the Fox* (New York: Harcourt, Brace & World, 1956); E.E. Robinson, *The Roosevelt Leadership, 1933–1945* (Philadelphia: Lippincott, 1955); W.E. Leuchtenburg, *F.D. Roosevelt and the New Deal, 1932–1940* (Roma-Bari: Laterza, 1976). Among the memoirs, see: F. Perkins, *The Roosevelt I Knew* (New York: Viking Press, 1946), and R.G. Tugwell, *The Democratic Roosevelt* (New York: Doubleday, 1957).

16. Cf. L. Ferrari Bravo, "Il New Deal e il nuovo assetto delle istituzioni capitalistiche," in Bologna et al., *Operai e stato.* Regarding the New Deal, we must necessarily make partial bibliographical references, not so much for the extent of literature the subject has produced, but because we intend to give priority to those references most directly relevant to the issues involved. For some general guidelines, however, in addition to the classics on the Great Depression cited in the present work (primarily Schlesinger, Bernstein, Leuchtenburg, Hofstadter, but others as well), see: C. Beard and, G.F. Smith, *The Old Deal and the New* (New York: Macmillan Co., 1940); Rauch, *History of the New Deal*; M. Einaudi, *The Roosevelt Revolution* (New York: Harcourt and Brace, 1959); E.C. Rozwenc ed., *The New Deal: Revolution or Evolution?*, Problems in American Civilization Series, Amherst College (Boston: D.C. Heath and Co.,1959); W. Davies, *The New Deal: Interpretations* (New York: Macmillan, 1964); O.L. Graham Jr., *The New Deal: The Critical Issues* (Boston: Little Brown and Co., 1971). Also the anthology edited by F. Mancini ed., *Il pensiero politico nell'età di Roosevelt* (Bologna: Il Mulino, 1962); M. Tronti, *Operai e capitale* (Torino: Einaudi, 1971); F. Villari, *Il New Deal* (Rome: Editori Riuniti, 1977).

Among the more recent releases in Italy, A. Duso ed., *Economia e istituzioni del New Deal* (Bari: De Donato, 1980), which collects the essays contained in *America's Recovery Program* (New York: Oxford University Press, 1934), trans. A. Cecconi; M. Telò ed., *Crisi e piano* (Bari: De Donato, 1979); Vaudagna, *Il New Deal* (in particular his introduction), and by the same author, "New Deal," in Bairati ed., *Storia del Nord America*, 262–297, and *Corporativismo e New Deal* (Torino: Rosenberg & Sellier, 1981).

Among more recent discussions, let us recall the seminar offered by the Gramsci Institute on "State and Capitalist Transformations in the 1930s" held in Frattocchie on November 18–19, 1978—in regard to this, see *Rinascita*, no. 48 (December 8, 1978): 13–26; the round table organized by *Il Manifesto*: "The 1930s of Our Day"—see *Il Manifesto* of December 2, 1978; the conference, "The Transformations of the Welfare State Between History and Future Prospecting," held in Turin, December 15–19, 1981, organized by the Piedmont Region, the Province of Turin, the city of Turin and the Lelio and Lisli Basso Foundation "ISSOCO."

17. It had been preceded by other urgent measures such as the Emergency Banking Act, the Economy Act, the establishment of the Civilian Conservation Corps, and the abandonment of the gold standard. It was soon followed by the Agricultiral Adjustment Act which called for a national agricultural policy, the Emergency Farm Mortgage Act which provided mortgages for financing agricultural property, the Tennessee Valley Authority Act that planned development in the Tennessee Valley, the Home Owners' Loan Act that provided the financing of mortgages on housing, and the National Industrial Recovery Act. For a detailed explanation of the content of these acts, and for more information on the relief provisions they offered, see the following: Schlesinger, *The Age of Roosevelt*; John P. Wernette, *Government and Business*; M. Fainsod, L. Gordon, and J.C. Palamountain Jr., *Government and the American Economy* (New York: Norton, [1941] 1948).

18. The FERA, however, did not deal directly with local public organizations. Half of the $500 million allocated was to be awarded as follows: one dollar from federal funds for every three dollars spent by each state for public aid during the previous three months. The other half was to be allocated where the needs were most urgent and the state was not able to cope even with its own share. Cf. Fainsod, Gordon, and Palamountain, *Government and the American Economy*, 771ff.

19. M. Capps, *Lotte per il salario: il Welfare Movement negli Stati Uniti negli anni sessanta* (typewritten), report presented at the conference held in January 1976 for the seminar I coordinated, "Women's Struggles and Policies of the Reproduction of Labor Power" (at the Institute of Social and Political Science at the University of Padua). This work gave me some ideas fundamental to the interpretation of welfare policy during the New Deal. For more information on the TVA, see: P. Selznick, *TVA and the Grass Roots: A Study in the Sociology of Formal Organization* (Berkeley: University of California Press, 1949), and W. Droze, *High Dams and Slack Waters: TVA Rebuilds a River* (Baton Rouge: Louisiana State University Press, 1965).

20. Books useful for data on measures of aid, public works, and social security include: J.L. Arnold, *The New Deal in the Suburbs: A History of the Greenbelt Town Program, 1935–1954* (Columbus: Ohio State University

Press, 1973); E.E. Witte, *The Development of the Social Security Act* (Madison: University of Wisconsin Press, 1962); J.F. Jones and J.M. Herrick, *Citizens in Service: Volunteers in Social Welfare During the Depression, 1929–1941* (East Lansing: Michigan State University Press, 1978); D. Nelson, *Unemployment Insurance: The American Experience, 1915–1935* (Madison: University of Wisconsin Press, 1969); J. Pechman et al., *Social Security: Perspectives for Reform* (Washington: Brookings, 1969); A.J. Altmeyer, *The Formative Years of Social Security* (Madison: University of Wisconsin Press, 1966).

128

For a remarkable testimony of one of the protagonists of welfare policy, see: H. Hopkins, *Spending to Save* (New York: W.W. Norton & Company, Inc., 1936); H. Ickes, *Back to Work: The Story of the PWA* (New York: The Macmillan Co., 1935); L. Meriam, *Relief and Social Security* (Washington: The Brookings Institution, 1946); E. Abbot, *Public Assistance* (Chicago: The University of Chicago Press, 1941); P.H. Douglas, *Social Security in the United States* (New York: Arno Press and The New York Times, [1936] 1971). We refer also to the authors already mentioned in Chapters Two and Three about unemployment. The study of aid and social security has garnered greater focus in recent years, while other aspects of the New Deal have received less scholarly attention.

21. J.M. Keynes, *The General Theory of Employment, Interest and Money* (London: Macmillan and Co., 1936), 116.

22. Schlesinger, *The Age of Roosevelt*, vol. II, 298. Cf. also: R.M. Fischer, *Twenty Years of Public Housing* (New York: Macmillan, 1959); C.L. Harris, *History and Policies of the Home Owners' Loan Corporation* (New York: Columbia University Press, 1951); T. McDonnell, *The Wagner Housing Act* (Chicago: Loyola University Press, 1957).

23. Based on the plans of the CWA, 500,000 kilometers of secondary roads were improved, 40,000 schools were built or improved, 50,000 teachers were employed, 500 airports were built and another 500 improved. They also built many parks, pools, canals, sewers, etc.

24. Schlesinger, *The Age of Roosevelt*, vol. II, 270.

25. Schlesinger, *The Age of Roosevelt*, vol. II, 304.

26. H. Pelling cited by Tronti, *Operai e capitale* (Torino: Einaudi, 1971), 297.

27. Cf. Capps, *Lotte per il salario*, and Fainsod, Gordon, and Palamountain, *Government and the American Economy*, 772ff.

28. In addition to the works already cited, see: R.J. Bunche, *The Political Status of the Negro in the Age of FDR* (Chicago and London: University of Chicago Press, 1973), 608ff.; B. Sternsher, *The Negro in Depression and War: Prelude to Revolution, 1930–1945* (Chicago: Quadrangle Books, 1969); B. Sitkoff, *New Deal for Blacks* (New York: Cambridge University Press, 1978); F.B. Walters, *Negroes and the Great Depression* (Westport, CT: Greenwood, 1970).

29. H.A. Millis and R.E. Montgomery, *The Economics of Labor*, vol. III, *Organized Labor* (New York and London: McGraw-Hill Book Co., 1945), 262–263. Cf. also J. Jacobson ed., *The Negro and the American Labor Movement* (New York: Anchor Books/Doubleday, 1968), and L. Valtz Mannucci, *I negri americani dalla depressione al dopoguerra* (Milan: Feltrinelli, 1974).

30. Jacobson, *Negro and the American Labor Movement*, 189.

31. Mannucci, *I negri americani dalla depressione al dopoguerra*, 13.

32. Frazier, *The Negro in the United States*, 601. Cf. also M.W. Kruman, "Quotas for Blacks: The Public Works Administration and the Black Construction Worker," *Labor History* 16 (1975): 37–51.

33. Frazier, *The Negro in the United States*, 601–602.

34. Ibid., 603.

35. Cf. J.A. Salmond, *Civilian Conservation Corps: 1933–1942, A New Deal Case Study* (Durham: Duke University Press, 1967).

36. Frazier, *The Negro in the United States*, 602–605. For further information on the initiatives discussed here, see Fainsod, Gordon, and Palamountain, *Government and the American Economy*.

37. Ibid., 272.

38. Ibid., 275.

39. Boone, *The Women's Trade Union Leagues*, says, "the problem of unemployed industrial women was particularly difficult, because they could not be fitted into work relief schemes as easily as white collar workers who could be used by government agencies." (195–196). For some reflections on public workers in the 1930s, cf. P. Bertella Farnetti, "Note sulla crisi del settore pubblico," in B. Cartosio ed., *Dentro l'America in crisi* (Bari: De Donato, 1980).

40. Schlesinger, *The Age of Roosevelt*, vol. II, 275.

41. Ibid., 274.

42. Ibid.

43. Ibid., 278. Cf. also Fainsod, Gordon, and Palamountain, *Government and the American Economy*, 772ff.

44. Schlesinger, *The Age of Roosevelt*, vol. II, 280–281. See also: A.W. MacMahon et al., *The Administration of Federal Work Relief* (Chicago: Public Administration Service, 1941), and D.S. Howard, *The WPA and Federal Relief Policy* (New York: Russel Sage Foundation, 1943).

45. Schlesinger, *The Age of Roosevelt*, vol. II, 287.

46. Ibid., 288.

47. Ibid., 290–291.

48. Ibid., 294.

49. Fainsod, Gordon, and Palamountain, *Government and the American Economy*, 773. Cf. also Piven and Cloward, *Regulating the Poor*, 109ff.

50. Analysis of the labor struggles of the 1930s is notoriously vast. For our part, the present work intends to deal with only essential references in

this aspect, and thus we limit ourselves to a few bibliographic references. In addition to the work by J.R. Commons already cited, which, however, only goes up to 1932, and the texts already referred to as classics on the Depression period, each with an extensive bibliography, it is still worth mentioning: M. Derber and E. Young eds., *Labor and the New Deal* (Madison: University of Wisconsin Press, 1957), including among its articles the famous essay by S. Perlman, "Labor and the New Deal in Historical Perspective"; J.R. Green, *The World of the Worker: Labor in Twentieth Century America* (New York: Hill & Wang, 1980); J. Bernstein, *The New Deal Collective Bargaining Policy* (Berkeley: University of California Press, 1950); M. Dubofsky, *American Labor since the New Deal* (Chicago: Quadrangle Books, 1971). For a review of more recent works in Italy, besides Tronti, *Operai e capitale*, see G. Romagnoli, "Il movimento degli scioperi negli Stati Uniti d'America, 1900–1970," in G.P. Cella ed., *Il movimento degli scioperi nel XX secolo* (Bologna: Il Mulino, 1979).

51. *National Industrial Recovery Act*, Title I, Sec. 7a.

52. Tronti, *Operai e capitale* (Torino: Einaudi, 1971), 286. See also G.P. Rawick, "Anni trenta: lotte operaie USA," in Bologna et al., *Operai e stato*.

53. H.A. Millis and E. Clark also state that between 1937, when the United States Supreme Court recognized the constitutionality of the Act, and 1947, at least 169 amendments to the Wagner Act were presented to Congress. *From the Wagner Act to Taft-Hartley* (Chicago: University of Chicago Press, 1950).

54. By the end of 1937 the CIO had 3,700,000 members and the AFL had 3,400,000. Among the members of the CIO there were 600,000 miners, 400,000 auto workers, 375,000 steel workers, 300,000 textile workers, 250,000 apparel workers, 100,000 workers in agricultural and the canning industry. On the role of the CIO, see: A. Preis, *Labor's Giant Step, Twenty Years of the CIO* (New York: Pathfinder Press, 1972); F. Ferrarotti, *Il dilemma dei sindacati americani* (Milan: Comunità, 1954), and by the same author, *Sindacati e potere negli Stati Uniti d'America* (Milan: Comunità, 1961); W. Galenson, *The CIO Challenge to the AFL* (Cambridge: Harvard University Press, 1960); J.M. Henever, *Which Side Are You On? The Harlan County Coal Miners, 1931–1939* (Urbana: University of Illinois Press, 1978); M. Dubofsky and W. Van Tine, *John L. Lewis: A Biography* (Chicago: Quandrangle Books, 1977); B. Ramirez, *When Workers Fight: The Politics of Industrial Relations in the Progressive Era, 1898–1916* (Westport, CT: Greenwood Press, 1978).

55. D. Montgomery in collaboration with R. Schatz, "Di fronte alle sospensioni di massa dal lavoro e alla disoccupazione," in D. Montgomery, *Rapporti di classe nell'America del primo 900* (Turin: Rosenberg & Sellier, 1980), 173.

56. Cf. Fainsod, Gordon, and Palamountain, *Government and the American Economy*; and Witte, *Development of the Social Security Act*.

57. Yoder, *Labor Economics and Labor Problems*, 317–325.

58. Fainsod, Gordon, and Palamountain, *Government and the American Economy*, 774.

59. Lubove, *The Struggle for Social Security*, 110ff.

60. The war in Vietnam, as shown through numerous interviews, gave Black women further determination to be paid wages for the production of children who they saw, overtly, destined for state interests in war or in the factory. On this matter, cf. M. Dalla Costa, "A proposito del welfare," *Primo Maggio*, nos. 9–10 (Winter 1977–78), and Milwaukee County Welfare Rights Organization, *Welfare Mothers Speak Out* (New York: W.W. Norton and Co., 1972).

61. A few indications of this can be found in the well known rise of illegitimate births, which also increasingly affected white women; in women's refusal to let public authorities know who their child's father was in order to receive aid; and in housing choices that coincided less with sentimental choices, especially in large cities.

62. Yoder, *Labor Economics and Labor Problems*, 376ff. The author estimates that in 1938, eleven million employees were covered by this Act and, among these, only 1,418,000 initially received less than 40 cents an hour. Cf. in this regard, M. Harrington, *The Other America: Poverty in the United States* (New York: Macmillan, 1969), 89. Commenting on the further legislative development of the Act under the Kennedy administration, Harrington notes that only about 20 percent of the 3.6 million workers covered by the law earned less than a dollar before it. So, again, legalizing it only slightly changed the actual situation.

CHAPTER 5

1. "If it is true that the New Deal programs were used to feed millions of needy Americans, they clamorously failed in the effort to restore full employment. Although in 1937 the gross national product had risen to levels roughly equal to those of 1929, the following year saw 10,400,000 people out of work, approximately nine million more than in 1929." D. Montgomery, "Di fronte alle sospensioni," 194.

2. See also *The Life and Times of Rosie the Riveter*, directed by Connie Field (USA, 1980, 65 mins), a documentary whose interest and novelty, even on a technical level, surpass many historical depictions of this period.

3. S. Fine, *Sit-down: The General Motors Strike of 1936–37* (Ann Arbor: The University of Michigan Press, 1969), 171

4. Brecher, *Strike!*, 198.

5. Fine, *Sit-down*, 201.

6. Ibid.

7. Ibid.

8. There are few studies on the struggles of women, and more generally, on the female condition in the 1930s. With regard to this strike we should

point out the reflections of S. Reverby, "With Babies and Banners: The Story of the Women's Emergency Brigade," in *Radical America*, vol. 13, no. 5 (September–October 1979).

9. Brecher, *Strike!*, 211. For the above examples and further information, see in particular chap. 5, part 3 (177–216).

10. Ibid., 211.

11. Ibid., 209.

12. Ibid.

13. Ibid. For other remarkable examples, see 207–209. For instance, the audacity of "450 employees at three De Met's tea rooms [who] sat down as 'the girls laughed and talked at the tables they had served' until they went home that night with a twenty-five percent pay increase"; and "About 150 women who had been serving meals in the company cafeteria engaged in a snake-dance, beating knives and forks against metal serving trays"; and the resolve of "Women [who] barricaded themselves in three tobacco plants for several weeks."

14. Ibid., 210–211.

15. Ibid., 182, 211: "These conflicts showed that ordinary people's lack of power over their daily lives led them to revolt not only in the workshops but in the rest of society as well."

16. In March of 1937, 170 industrial occupations were officially reported. Undoubtedly there were many more. See Fine, *Sit-down*, 331.

17. Wandersee, *Women's Work and Family Values*, 89.

18. Census Bureau, *Occupation Statistics*, p. 8, and "Census Bureau Release," October 28, 1938. The data from these reports is discussed in Yoder, *Labor Economics and Labor Problems*, 353. For more information on the characteristics of female employment, see 347–381.

19. See Milkman, "Women's Work and the Economic Crisis."

20. For the above data, cf. Wandersee, *Women's Work and Family Values*, 86–87.

21. Yoder, *Labor Economics and Labor Problems*, 360ff.

22. Ibid.

23. Schlesinger, *The Age of Roosevelt*, vol. II, 90.

24. Baker, *Technology and Woman's Work*, 404–405.

25. It is estimated that in 1920, there were 396,000 women enrolled in the AFL, and in 1938, the female members of the CIO numbered approximately 700,000 to 800,000. This proportion is still low compared to the numbers of working women. Yoder, *Labor Economics and Labor Problems*, 364. Cf. also Wolman, *The Growth of American Trade Unions*, from which Yoder draws information on women's unionization in 1920.

26. Wandersee, *Women's Work and Family Values*, 97.

27. Smuts, *Women and Work in America*, 145. Cf. also Chafe, *The American Woman*, 107–109.

28. Chafe, *The American Woman*, 108.

29. Wandersee, *Women's Work and Family Values*, 91.

30. Ibid., 77–79, including data of the 6th census of 1940.

31. Chafe, *The American Woman*, 107.

32. Wandersee, *Women's Work and Family Values*, 68ff.

33. Ibid., 53.

34. Ibid., 99.

35. Ibid., 27.

36. Boone, *The Women's Trade Union Leagues*, chap. 8.

37. Ibid., 195–196.

38. Ibid., 200.

39. Ibid., 200–201. A. Tunc and S. Tunc, *Le système constitutionnel des États Unis d'Amérique*, 2 vols. (Paris: Domat, 1954). Cf. E.S. Redford, *American Government and the Economy* (New York: Macmillan, 1965), chap. 13–14. On the Supreme Court, see S. Volterra, "Corte suprema," in Bairati ed., *Storia del Nord America*, 15–30.

40. Boone, *The Women's Trade Union Leagues*, 202.

41. Cf. Yoder, *Labor Economics and Labor Problems*, 365ff.

42. Boone, *The Women's Trade Union Leagues*, 209.

43. Ibid., 213.

44. Cf. Wandersee, *Women's Work and Family Values*, 92–97.

45. In 1937 there were 288 clinics in 40 states and the District of Columbia. Birth control, however, was only partially attributable to the use of contraceptives. Not only were such means still few, their use was largely opposed. Proletarian women had less chance to have birth control prescribed by doctors who could move between the folds of the various laws. While Margaret Sanger, president of the Birth Control League—which she founded in 1921, and which would become the Planned Parenthood Federation of America in 1941—continued to fight for birth control, the famous case of the United States v. One Package broke out in 1936 as a result of the seizure at customs of a package of diaphragms that Dr. Hannah Stone had imported from Japan. The same year saw the publication of N.E. Himes' *Medical History in Contraception* (New York: Gamut Press).

46. Wandersee, *Women's Work and Family Values*, 55.

47. Cf. H.E. Mower, *Personality Adjustment and Domestic Discord* (New York: American Books, 1935).

48. A.C. Kinsey, *Sexual Behavior in the Human Male* (Philadelphia: Saunders Co., 1948); Kinsey, *Sexual Behavior in the Human Female* (Philadelphia: Saunders Co., 1953). One should recall that the 1920s and early 1930s were the years when, after the advance of empirical social research, works that marked the transition to a complete change in the framework of American sociology appeared.

49. Commercial advertising, and even Hollywood movies, were important tools for disseminating patterns of behavior originally developed for the

middle class among proletarian women. On the role of advertising, cf. S. Ewen, *Captains of Consciousness* (New York: McGraw-Hill, 1977); on the role of cinema, see: B. Cartosio, *Tute e technicolor*; L. Rosten, *Hollywood: The Movie Colony, The Movie Makers* (New York: Harcourt, Brace & Co., 1941); R. Sklar, *Cinemamerica* (Milan: Feltrinelli, 1982); L. May, *Screening Out the Past* (New York: Oxford University Press, 1980).

50. Cf. G. Ciucci, F. Dal Co, M. Manieri-Elia and M. Tafuri, *La città americana dalla guerra civile al New Deal* (Rome-Bari: Laterza, 1973), 275ff.

51. D. Calabi, "Politica della casa e ricerca urbanistica," in U. Curi ed., *Tendenze della ricerca americana 1900–1940* (Venice: Istituto Gramsci, Sezione Veneta, 1976), 72–73. For a more comprehensive discussion, see L. Mumford, *The City in History* (New York: Harcourt, Brace & World, 1961).

52. S. Giedion, *Mechanization Takes Command*, 564–566.

53. Ibid., 490, 564.

54. Ibid., 555ff.

55. D. Montgomery, "Di fronte alle sospensioni," recalling how collaboration during the First World War between business, academia, and the military laid the groundwork for further coordination between universities and companies that was no longer limited to the field of engineering but extended to the humanities, observes that the current campaign of big industries and foundations for the creation of "private initiative" teaching posts in American universities appears to be a real desire to be the best (see 189ff.).

APPENDIX

1. Milwaukee County Welfare Rights Organization, *Welfare Mothers Speak Out: We Ain't Gonna Shuffle Anymore* (New York: W.W. Norton & Co., 1972).

2. *Primo Maggio 6* (Winter 1975–1976): 8.

3. Ibid., 18.

4. Ibid., 19.

5. Ibid., 3.

6. Beyond the monthly allowance (calculated on the basis of the number of family members), the principal expression of welfare lies in the category of 'special needs,' which allows access to money for 'emergency cases,' among other things, and which is to be used for acquiring new furniture, clothing, and books for children, etc. It was on this basis that women were able to wage an ongoing struggle for more money. And, not by accident, it is this category that will be the first victim of all the welfare reforms introduced since the early 1960s. It was also in this period that welfare came to be presented as a 'flat grant,' that is, as a fixed sum that is meant to cover all of the family's needs.

7. Cf. Daniel Moynihan, *The Politics of a Guaranteed Income* (New York: Vintage Books, 1973).

8. None of which removes the fact that in the last two years the number of recipients of Home Relief, who used to represent a minority, has exploded. In fact, it is only due to the great wave of unemployment that struck the East Coast in particular that New York City was forced to concede Home Relief to all of the unemployed whose support had run out. Home Relief, to be precise, is a non-federal category of welfare and exists at the discretion of local authorities. In fact, it exists only in New York City and a few other cities. It consists of money provided to those who can demonstrate that they have no income and cannot find work.

9. Moynihan, *The Politics of a Guaranteed Income*, 82–83.

10. Ibid., 29.

11. Ibid., 66.

12. Cf. Heather Ross, *Poverty: Women and Children Last* (Washington, DC: Urban Institute, 1976), 11.

13. Ibid., 5. In relation to this, also see: Joint Economic Committee, *Studies in Public Welfare*, Paper no. 12, part 1, "The Family, Poverty and Welfare Programs: Factors Influencing Family Instability" (Washington, DC: U.S. Government Printing Office, 1973), esp. 154. One can not only calculate that today the number of divorces has increased by 60 percent since 1965, but that one in three marriages end in divorce.

14. *Primo Maggio* 6, 3.

15. It was exactly because of the refusal of the young to 'serve their country' that the American government has been forced to turn into a voluntary army for some years now.

16. *Primo Maggio* 6, 19.

17. "City Opens Computer Center to Check on Eligibility of Welfare Recipients," *New York Times*, February 28, 1975.

18. Cf. Moynihan, *The Politics of a Guaranteed Income*, which centers on an analysis of the FAP.

19. "Welfare," *Robert MacNeil Report*, July 7, 1976.

20. On the federalization of welfare projects, cf. "The Welfare State and the Public Welfare," *Fortune*, June 1976. The proposal for the federalization of welfare paves the way for the homogenization of quotas on a national level (the quantitative quota currently varies from state to state). This 'homogenization' will of course not be achieved on the basis of areas where the cost of living is the highest but where it is lowest, as has already been shown in the case of SSI.

21. In fact, centralization means the reduction of offices—welfare centers— that have until now always been the nerve centers of daily conflict.

22. It is telling that Carter's economists, who made this reform the flagship policy of his electoral campaign, recently announced that a full reform would not be possible before 1980.

23. Beginning on February 16, 1977, a new form had to be filled out by

women on welfare declaring where the father of their children resided, so that the state could track him down. They also had to divulge whether they had had any other sexual relationships at the time of conception. A "wise" about-turn from the days when it was necessary to hide any trace of a man at home in order to maintain welfare support.

24. "Social Security Numbers Will Track Runaway Fathers," *New York Times*, April 7, 1976.

25. This proposal has been subject to a vast amount of criticism from American parents, who have seen it as an attempt at 'Sovietization' of child rearing; see "A Twisted Attack on Day Care," *Newsday*, January 30, 1976, which, despite the sensationalist title, highlights its merits.

ACKNOWLEDGEMENTS

This work makes use of numerous discussions with Maurizio Vaudagna on some aspects of unionization, with Peppino Ortoleva on Progressivism and the movement of the unemployed, with Sara Volterra for jurisprudence and legislation, with Marina Schenkel and Hilary Creek for some aspects of labor supply. Bruno Cartosio also provided me with important information. Silvia Federici and George Caffentzis, whom I worked with closely in New York, continued, as always, to give me advice and materials even after my return to Italy. Others have consistently helped in the process of this book's completion, allowing me constant comparison and verification. This list includes Valeria Fusetti, Dario De Bortoli, Julian Bees, Tino Costa, Nino Capodaglio, M.G. and A.M., to whom, while respecting their desire for anonymity, I reaffirm my deep gratitude. To all I extend my heartfelt thanks, apologizing in advance for not having been an adequate interpreter of all the suggestions I received. I also want to give a deeply felt thank you to my mother, Maria Ghidelli, who, with great love, consistently supported my material and immaterial reproduction in the difficult years when I wrote this book.

ABOUT THE AUTHOR AND CONTRIBUTORS

MARIAROSA DALLA COSTA is an influential author and international feminist who has devoted her theoretical and practical efforts to the study of the female condition in capitalist development. Starting with Potere Operaio, Lotta Femminista, and the International Wages for Housework Campaign, Dalla Costa has for decades been a central figure in the development of autonomy in a wide range of anticapitalist movements. Her seminal book *The Power of Women and the Subversion of the Community*, coauthored with Selma James, has been translated into six languages. Her writings, reflecting on the role of social reproduction in the organization of autonomy as well as the historic development of capital, have consistently been staged within and through social struggles and movements organizing around the questions of land, agriculture, food, and the commons.

Dalla Costa's writings have been published in English, Spanish, Portuguese, French, German, Turkish, Korean, Greek, and Japanese. Many of her articles are available in *The Commoner* (www.commoner.org). Her English publications include *Women, Development and Labor of Reproduction*, coedited with G.F. Dalla Costa, and *Gynocide, Hysterectomy, Capitalist Patriarchy and the Medical Abuse of Women*, as well as *Our Mother Ocean: Enclosures, Commons, and World Fishermen's Movement*. An anthology of her writings, *Women and the Subversion of the Community*, was published in 2019.

Mariarosa Dalla Costa previously taught at the Department of Political and Juridical Science and International Studies at the University of Padua, Italy.

SILVIA FEDERICI is a critically acclaimed feminist, Marxist theorist, and author of *Caliban and the Witch*, *Revolution at Point Zero*, and *Witches, Witch-Hunting, and Women*, among others. She is also coeditor of *Feminicide and Global Accumulation*, with Liz Mason-Deese and Susana Draper.

LIZ MASON-DEESE is a feminist translator and part of the translation collective Territorio de Ideas, an editor of *Viewpoint Magazine*, and a longtime participant in feminist and anticapitalist movements in Argentina.

ABOUT THE ARCHIVE OF FEMINIST STRUGGLE FOR WAGES FOR HOUSEWORK

The Archive of Feminist Struggle for Wages for Housework contains a wealth of material collected from the 1970s to the present, graciously donated by Mariarosa Dalla Costa after years of work as a militant in the feminist movement and as a scholar of the condition of women. The archive, based in Padua, Italy, collects a range of inventoried material from a strand of the feminist movement with an international, militant, anticapitalist dimension. In Italy, this movement first called itself *Movimento di Lotta Femminile* [Women's Struggle Movement], then later *Lotta Femminista* [Feminist Struggle] and finally *Movimento dei Gruppi e Comitati per il Salario al Lavoro Domestico* [Movement of Groups and Committees for Wages for Housework].

The Archive's address and contact information is:

Archivio di Lotta Femminista per il salario al lavoro domestic
Biblioteca Civica
Centro Culturale San Gaetano
Via Altinate 71, 35121
Padova, Italy

Consultation Hours
Monday and Thursday, 8:30am to 5:30pm
Phone: + 39 049 820 4811, Fax +39 049 820 4804
Email: biblioteca.civica@comune.padova.it

COMMON NOTIONS is a publishing house and programming machine that fosters the collective formulation of new directions for living autonomy in everyday life.

We aim to translate, produce, and circulate tools of knowledge production utilized in movement-building practices. Through a variety of media, we seek to generalize common notions about the creation of other worlds beyond state and capital.

Our publications include:

Mariarosa Dalla Costa and Monica Chilese, *Our Mother Ocean: Enclosure, Commons, and the Global Fishermen's Movement* (978-1-942173-00-7, $15.95)

Silvia Federici, Susana Draper, and Liz Mason-Deese, editors, *Feminicide and Global Accumulation: Frontline Struggles to Resist the Violence of Patriarchy and Capitalism* (978-1942173-44-1, $20)

CareNotes Collective, *For Health Autonomy: Horizons of Care Beyond Austerity* (978-1-942173-14-4, $15)

Mario Tronti and Andrew Anastasi, editor and translator, *Weapon of Organization: Mario Tonti's Political Revolution in Marxism* (978-1-942173-22-9, $20)

CounterPower, *Organizing for Autonomy: History, Theory, and Strategy for Collective Liberation* (978-1-942173-21-2, $20)

The Red Nation, *The Red Deal: Indigenous Action to Save Our Earth* (978-1942173-43-4, $15)

www.commonnotions.org
info@commonnotions.org